CW00832483

Oh All Right Then

MARJORY A MACLEAN

Copyright © 2024 Marjory A MacLean

All rights reserved.

ISBN: 9798322995302

CONTENTS

Many of the chapters are followed by sermons, each preached at some point along my way and suggested by one of the themes of that chapter.

Also by Marjory MacLean

As author:
The Crown Rights of the Redeemer 2009
Speaking from the Heart 2010
Visions and Authorities 2023

As editor:
The Legal Systems of Scottish Churches 2009
The Naval Church Service Book 2011

A NOTE ABOUT THE TITLE

I had a fascinating little debate with the friend who proof-read this book for me. She wanted to put a comma after 'Oh' in the title. And when I pressed her, I realised that she was hearing it in her head as 'Oh! (surprise) *All* right then! (agreement)'

No , I need you to read it as if through gritted teeth, all in a rush, with the emphasis on '*right*', as if you are a reluctant teenager losing the argument about tidying your room.

If you watch the video (see next note) you'll get it.

A NOTE ABOUT A VIDEO

As I read a biography or even a novel, I often wish I could hear the author's actual voice, hear the words as they would sound if spoken by their writer.

So I've taken the liberty of making a little video of the text of the Introduction that follows this page. The printed version and the video are the same words; so if you're not an internetty type, just turn the page now and get on with the book. If, though, you wonder what this crazy lady looks and sounds like, go onto YouTube, find 'Marjory MacLean' in its internal search, and start typing 'Oh All Right Then' until you see the video. After you've watched it, you can start reading again at chapter 1 and save yourself the next few pages.

As you prefer **...**

INTRODUCTION

Oh all right then.

I am sitting on top of those cliffs you can see on the front cover of the book, at Yesnaby in Orkney. It is early in 1986, I am not quite half way through my two-year solicitor's traineeship with Messrs TP&JL Low in Kirkwall, and I've come to my favourite weekend walking place with a sense that I have a decision to make.

Yesnaby, let me say in case you've never been there, is a place for decisions. If any of you intends ever to propose marriage to me, do it at Yesnaby. I know nowhere more beautiful and awe-inspiring, and nowhere that more assures me of the relentlessness of the activity of God in our world. I know that in the middle of the night when no-one is there, those waves will keep crunching into those caves and sending spray over onto the lichen carpet along the top of those terrifying drops. Being put in my tiny place by that power so far beyond my controlling gives me a sense that my part in all this is so small that I really shouldn't fret about it.

A decision is due for this not-quite-24-year-old baby lawyer. The uncomfortable process I'll describe in the next chapter has taken me, over five years, to the point at which the 'plan A' version of my imagined future is parish ministry in the Church of Scotland. To plan a journey, though, is not the same thing as switching on the ignition; and to imagine being a minister is not the same thing as saying it out loud to the Church and beginning the process.

I can still say No. I can still take the easier path, stay in a place I thoroughly enjoy. I can still occupy the profession my parents have supported me in entering, my parents whose attitude at this point is, 'Why would you give up something secure that you know, and change to something that might end up being a disaster?' (Though fast forward seven or eight years, and to their credit they say 'You were right, we see that now'.)

If I say Yes at this point, the next step will be one of application, assessment and decision by the Church itself, and that involves being vulnerable to incisive questioning and testing, and the risk of not hearing the answer I want. That will then require me to work out what 'plan B' is for my professional life, and it will also take quite a bit out of me emotionally. So Yes is the harder path, but it's the one I feel is stretching out in front of me and I have to find out where it goes.

Oh all right then, almost drowned out by the crump of water on stone below... but no doubt heard all the same.

That exclamation, or something like it, must be the turning-point of every life that ends up in Christian ministry. And after that it's like setting foot on a playground slide on an icy day: no stopping and little control and who knows where I'm going to end up. And all of that 'ending up' is what this book will try to describe.

For more than half the length of my ministry, people have listened to me telling some story in which I am the foolish anti-hero, and have responded by saying I ought to write my stories down, write 'the book'. Until now I have resisted their flattery for two reasons. First, so many of the stories also involve other people as protagonists that it could be difficult – I have often joked – to avoid defamation suits; there are other ministers almost as hapless as I am but they may not want that to become known. Second, I cannot imagine that it is a good use of anyone's time to be reading a biography of this muddle of a soul, nor would I want my life to be commended as an example of anything much.

But recently I had reason to see the reading-list given to those going through our current process of discernment of vocation, and realised that its compilers (no fault of theirs) had been provided with very little that was directly useful to members of the Church of Scotland. It suddenly seemed to me that if I wrote 'the book', but making it clear that its subject is 'the ministry' and not one particular minister, I might be able to plug a little of that gap. The privileges, adventures and errors of my 30+ years of ordained service will be the quarry of examples I will use; and so you will probably learn things about me you didn't know you needed to know – sorry about that. (And I figure I can probably confine myself to stories in which the other characters look good, so I won't worry about that after all.)

Those in discernment for our ministry, then, are one target readership for this little volume. Another is much more numerous, and it's the members of our Church who would like to find out a bit more about the mysterious topic of what it is their minister is actually doing, and celebrate the work of the whole ministry of the denomination they call their kirk, and take some pride and pleasure in being part of Christ's Church reaching into so many nooks and crannies of life in Scotland and beyond.

Bottom Line Up Front, as they say in the world of slick corporate presentations. Here is the nutshell argument of everything you are about to read.

The ordained ministry of the Church of Scotland (and I dare say of any denomination) is the most extraordinarily varied life, which is only as limited as your imagination and desire make it. I have lost count of the pickles in which I've found myself thinking 'New College didn't think to prepare me for this', and almost all of those pickles are ones I am – well, in retrospect – glad I experienced.

The corollary of that truth is that to be a fully functioning, mentally healthy minister you need to bring a variety of skills and gifts, not knowing which of them you will use from moment to moment. Piety is grand, but not enough; and the talents you have been given will serve you well, sometime, somehow.

If that speaks of an adaptibility, it means you will also need to be open to being changed by the experience. In part, that's about the readiness to attend to all those different demands and unexpected scenarios. In part, it's about the willingness to be affected, changed, re-orientated by your formation for ministry and your experience of the work. In part, whether we like it or not, it's about the realism of knowing that we minister in a Church that is drastically changing and shrinking, in which we need to maintain our confidence, keep the faith and follow the vocation through.

Some of the topics that follow will interest you more than others, so let me give you the time-line I have used to arrange the chapters that follow, in case you want to focus on a particular one.[1]

1986, June (the month in which I turned 24) – completed the Church's selection process (Chapter 1 *Vocation*)
1987-90 – studied for Bachelor of Divinity degree at New College, Edinburgh. (2 *Formation for Ministry*)

[1] This might be a sensible place to offer a warning. Processes and terminology change from time to time in our Church, and I'll always be using the language that was current at the time of the event I describe. So for instance, the selection process of the 1980s was less sophisticated than the current one; and the BD degree was done by candidates who were already graduates in other disciplines, which is no longer the case. Parish names are constantly changing, and I may refer to Presbyteries that no longer exist. Be patient, and don't treat any of it as accurate in today's world.

1990-92 – probationary period, and then ordained assistantship, Fairmilehead, Edinburgh (2)
1992-98 – minister of Stromness and Graemsay, Orkney (3 *Stromness and Graemsay*)
During this ministry I also served as part-time Depute Clerk of the General Assembly from 1996 (4 *121 and the General Assembly*)
1998-2010 – full-time Depute Clerk (4)
During this appointment I studied part-time for a PhD from New College. (5 *Studying, Thinking, Speaking, Writing*)
After that I joined the Royal Naval Reserve as a chaplain. (6 *Royal Naval Reserve*)
2010-11 – mobilised as a chaplain in the Royal Navy (6)
2011-2020 – minister of (i) Abernyte linked with (ii) Inchture and Kinnaird linked with (iii) Longforgan, in Dundee Presbytery (7 *The Carse of Gowrie*)
During this ministry I continued to serve in the RNR until 2017 (my 55th birthday), and held various committee memberships and convenerships within the Church's governance structures. (8 *Miscellaneous Thoughts*)
2020-date – minister of South Ronaldsay and Burray, Orkney (9 *SRB and HW*)
At the time of writing I am Interim Moderator of Hoy and Walls, and anticipate these two parishes being brought together in a more organic way in a Team Ministry being planned for Orkney in October 2024.

Right then. I promised stories of things the University of Edinburgh did not prepare me to experience. So let me start with one of those 'you couldn't make this up' moments, one that happened just before Christmas 2023. Like all of my stories in the coming pages, it's not hilarious; it's just a memorable little episode.

As part of those radical changes we're all enduring in the Church, the wise and brave Kirk Session of Hoy and Walls Parish had taken the necessary steps to divest the Church of its last historic church building there, and consolidate all the worship and activity in the modern bungalow known as Kirkside that stands in the curtilege of the original building. Disciplined decisions were taken about the destination of the contents of the church: the communion table was already in Kirkside's brand-new conservatory, the memorial plaque for the 1969 Longhope Lifeboat Disaster was destined for the Lifeboat Museum nearby, and wood from a pew once sat on by HM the Queen Mother would be fashioned into a table-top lectern.

That left the font, the early twentieth century, much-loved, generously-gifted and – this is the critical point – sandstone font. I'll show you a picture of it in a minute. It is a work of art and a treasured artefact resonating with generations of worship; but you won't think me crass if I say that one of the most positive things you can also say about it is that it was made in two octagonal sections, one sitting flush on top of the other. Thank goodness for that.

When Kirkside had been extended to include the conservatory, the local builder was asked to ensure that the floor of the new area would be strong enough to take a very heavy weight in one corner. Ask me in a few years whether his assurances were vindicated; it may take some time to know for sure. For that, it was decided, would be the destination of the font. But how to move it, on a small island with a population of only 450 and no engineering firms? Half in jest, someone wondered whether the Lifeboat crew might appreciate a training exercise, but such a ridiculous notion was left hanging in the air.

There I was then, in mid Advent, spending a few nights in the house to do some Christmassy services and pastoral visits. 'Oh, by the way', said one of the Session (note to future ministers, that's usually a warning signal for something bad or mad, just saying), 'the Fire Brigade will call round after teatime tomorrow'.

Well, it took the six of them three quarters of an hour to move the thing about 30 yards, slinging each half below scaffolding poles with straps and ropes and clever knots, trundling it on rollers across the parking space, squeezing through the conservatory door, and putting all their back-muscles on the line to hoist the top bit onto the bottom bit and then get the eight corners aligned.

The Session Clerk (aged 90, so definitely exempt) and I (aged 61 and determined to be exempt too) stood back making encouraging noises. A voice came out of the scrum of effort, 'Promise us neither of you intends ever to move this again'.

That, dear Reader, is what being a Church of Scotland minister feels like. I hope you enjoy the other gentle stories I have to tell you.

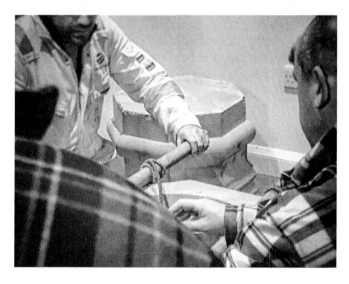

Kirkside font being installed, December 2023

1 VOCATION

Now it's October 1980, the beginning of the first term of my first year as a law student at Edinburgh University's Old College. A formal academic service to mark the beginning of the new session is taking place in St Giles' Cathedral, and in my desire to acquire what I assume is the fullness of the university experience I have come along, and I'm sitting towards the west end facing towards the communion table far away under the east window. (If you know St Giles', that dates this story to a point before the re-orientation of the church around the crossing as it is today.)

Various clergy are assembling to join the academic procession; and my eye falls on two of them, and they are women.[2] And at that point my heart sinks like a stone. In my eighteen-year lifetime of Church attendance, five of them as a communicant member, it has never occurred to

---

[2] Helen Alexander, then the new probationer and a superb practitioner of public prayer, went on to serve St Giles' with immense grace and flair at both ends of her ministerial career. Nancy Norman, an American member of the staff team with a marvellously wicked laugh, ended up as a Church of Scotland minister serving in Peeblesshire and later in South Lanarkshire.

me that women might be eligible to serve as ministers.[3] It has, consequently, never occurred to me that I might be eligible to wonder whether I should serve as a minister. Here, in an instant, in a strange church, just too far into the first term to change course, I am facing the real solution to a puzzle I thought I had solved.

As a secondary school pupil, I was fairly good at everything on the humanities side of the curriculum and found the maths and science side more of a chore. I didn't excel extremely in any one subject; the only academic prize I won in Forfar Academy was a share of the Latin prize in S3, and nothing after that. I felt, though, that I wanted to pursue something professional and vocational, and knew I had some skills in public speaking and a willingness to serve the communities in which I was set (which included the Church).

In my brain, and limited by what I didn't know I didn't know, it felt to me as if I was being pointed towards the law. My puzzled family, devoid of lawyers on either side and in any generation, nonetheless supported and encouraged me... and could see how I had come to that conclusion. The law is a profession that suits people with an interest in philosophical ideas and conceptual thinking, with skill in presenting arguments convincingly, with a passion to help people in the most dramatic and difficult episodes of their lives. The law is a profession where it helps if you don't mind a bit of ceremonial, some distinctive (if historical) working dress, gracious surroundings for people's most significant life events...

Yes, I *know*. But then, remember, I *didn't* know what I didn't know!

---

[3] The legislation declaring the eligibility of women to be ordained as ministers was finally passed by the General Assembly in 1968, two years after similar legislation in relation to the eldership. I was born in 1962 and brought up in Forfar where – through no-one's fault or mischief I am sure – ministers were men throughout my childhood and teenage years. And if you don't know that pink hippopotami exist, there is nothing that prompts you to ask whether they do.

OH ALL RIGHT THEN

So there I was, my bright new folders and unbashed textbooks on things like Family Law, the Scottish Legal System, and Roman Law back in my bedroom in my Hall of Residence, sitting in St Giles' with the blood draining to my feet and feeling as if I might just have stepped through a door that wasn't the right one.

It seemed that the very least I should demand of those women who were unwittingly causing me a crisis was to meet and talk. The advice I was given then was what anyone my age would have been told in those days when there was no shortage of applicants for ordination. I should proceed with the degree course I had begun, mature a bit, learn more about the life of the Church, and see how my sense of vocation might develop. Today, when enquirers tend to be middle-aged and considering a late career-change, that advice would not be given in the same terms... and quite right too.

As I look back over the ministry I've had so far, I can see the smiling face of Providence in that conversation. While it takes seven years to qualify as a solicitor in Scotland, and so I was being treated a little like poor old Jacob when he tried to marry his first love and was denied her, the long path I followed enabled me in the fullness of a lot of time to give my individual and distinctive service to the Church far into the teenage me's future. I am glad I swallowed hard and continued with my Old College course.

Mind you, I allowed the tumult of what we would nowadays term 'discernment' to influence the shape and content of that law degree. Assuming that a career in law would remain my backup plan if ministry didn't work out, I obediently scraped my way through the professional subjects I would need to pass to enter the Scottish legal world, things like Criminal Law, Delict, Contract and so on. Then when it came to Honours options, when most students were taking those skills up to a higher standard, I bailed out completely and opted for things like Criminology, European Legal History and various elements of Legal

Philosophy ('jurisprudence' in that sense). I suppose I was turning a law degree into something as much like a more general humanities degree as I could, to serve as an intellectual foundation on which to add a theological training later on.

Four years of LLB and a year's Diploma in Legal Practice later, I only needed to complete the two-year traineeship to become fully qualified, and figuratively to put *that* profession into my back pocket while I explored *this* troublesome sense of a very different vocation. By this time I suspected that, whatever happened, I was unlikely to remain in the legal profession forever, and so I burned another small boat. I decided not to worry about finding a traineeship in one of the prestigious firms in Edinburgh or Glasgow (the kind of launchpad from which it is easier to find one's way to the Scottish Bar, for instance), since I really didn't think I was going to propel myself into any legal heights. Instead, I decided, I would treat myself to two years in the nicest place I could find to live and work, somewhere in which I could reflect in peace on the inner storm of my head, somewhere that would be a place to make decisions. My mother rather naughtily added, 'Make it somewhere that will be nice for holidays for your father and me.'

And that is how I ended up in that moment on the Yesnaby cliff-top five and a half years after the one in St Giles', with a perfectly good career beckoning, an interest in various alternatives outside of the Church, and yet the draw of this one idea that was pulling harder than the others.

What, then, are we discerning, we who go through a process like the one I've just narrated or the thousand completely different narrations you would hear from the first thousand clergy you randomly asked to tell you their story?

Well, it's a sense of (1) being called (2) to do or be something, isn't it? Let me start with the second of those, since you need to know what the 'something' is before you can judge whether it's your 'calling'.

What are you imagining the ministry to be, as you consider whether it lies in your future? Or, for readers with a more general interest in the Church and her ways, what is your minister for? If you follow the thread of ecclesiastical history, you will find many attempts, some of them quite formal and official, to define that. There are more theological-sounding definitions, in terms of preaching, pastoral care, sacramental ministry and the exercise of discipline. There are more structural definitions, as the Church in recent times has set out in handbooks and guidance the sorts of responsibilities a minister has and the sort of thoughtful and reflective approach that should be used. There are what you might call charismatic definitions, individual examples of such inspiring commitment or achievement or oratory or insight that a good model for ministry can be built simply by emulating that other's great life.

Maybe we all ought to keep reflecting on those sorts of ideals of ministry throughout our attempts to practise this profession. I suspect most of us don't. I suspect most of us come, over the years, to define ministry according to the pattern it has created in our weekly or yearly calendars. At the end of each week I copy next week's appointments from my electronic diary into an A4 desk diary, and mark off also my non-work time. In the space that remains I slot in the elements of preparation of worship: a couple of half-mornings for a sermon, another for the other elements of the service, a bit of time for church-related social media posting and the preparation of Sunday's powerpoint if one will be needed. Then I find the space that is left for visiting (where I am at the moment, I find I normally have enough – many ministers struggle with this), and I create the space I need for the miscellaneous and the one-off: my turn to write the holy column for the local paper, some opening worship for a meeting I'm chairing, a tricky conversation to be had with someone feeling grumpy about something, arrangements to make for a special event, and the rest. And with that exercise – I call it 'diarising' – done before the week begins, I am as confident as I can be that I'll arrive at each engagement ready to be articulate and briefed on all possible outcomes. But it means my understanding of the larger question of what I'm here to do is rather running on rails, defined by habit.

Growing old can be wonderfully liberating in ministry, as there's less of a future progress to plot and plan, and so you can allow things to become much more simple. If I'm spared to work until I'm about 70, then I'm now slightly more than three-quarters of the way through my ministry; and at this stage I've figured out at long last three things that I'm for—and all the preaching and visiting and administering and turning up at events is just 'how' I do those three things. I list them in no particular order, as I think they are equally interesting.

First, I exist to love the communities in which I am set. I am a notoriously unsentimental person, and so by 'love' I mean something practical, understanding, inclusive, available, generous, rational, purposeful, and not something gooey, tearful, hysterical. When someone in the community has suffered a tragic bereavement, family and friends will call round or get in touch with all their own emotion on show and no wonder. That sharing of outward grief is a healthy part of a supported loving process. It is also true, though, that one of the things that bereaved person needs is the presence of the professional who brings that more clear-eyed kind of loving service – whether that is the GP, the undertaker or the minister – giving something to hang onto that isn't wobbling. And that same kind of love is needed too for the person who has just done something terrible, or just been the victim of something horrifying, or just suffered the devastation of a relationship or family splitting apart. Not 'tough' love (which means something else), but 'strong' love of a particular kind that takes training and practice.

St Augustine, preaching on St John's first letter, said 'Love, and do what you want'. If I am loving 'my' people, I can probably follow my instincts in my other decisions about ministry, even if that makes a terrible mess of next week's diary, even if *that* is a prospect that makes me shudder a little as I even type the words.

Second, I am here to pray. Obviously that involves interceding for my congregations, for the communities they serve, and especially for individuals I know whose needs are particularly acute. This is not the place to go into the theology of prayer and how you think it 'works'. Even if those for whom I pray don't know that I'm doing it, or don't believe that it would directly change anything for them, I adhere to the belief that the doing of it matters, if only as part of the love I've been describing. It touches me to know someone is praying for me, and it touches me to think they were doing it before I discovered that they were doing it, and my being touched like that is some sort of caress, surely, that 'gentles' me – if I may be permitted to make that word a verb.

It's not just about intercession though. Doesn't it mean something that at the heart of a faith community there is someone educated, skilled and dedicated who is trying to practise the presence of God, to discern what is meant by 'thy will be done', who is daily bringing supplication for better insight to share? Anyone can pray in these ways of course, and in principle everyone should. A minister is not there to pray vicariously for everyone else and save the congregation the 'bother' of doing it for themselves. I mean, rather, that a minister brings all the bits and pieces of their education, experience, wisdom and love into their prayers, and there is something unique about that which rightly belongs somewhere close to the middle of the life of the worshipping community.

OH ALL RIGHT THEN

Third, I am here to remember people's souls. I mean I am here to remember that everyone I meet *has* a soul, a core that is not confined to the span of this life, an identity that is fundamentally loved and redeemed and called and safe. If a person consists of something more than body, mind and emotions, and if their road does not run only through this world, that changes how they will see themselves and how others will see them. Perhaps things have gone so wrong that their only hope is to encounter the one community that tries to believe that nothing in this world is unforgiveable. Perhaps they are so broken in their health that they need to feel they belong in a realm beyond this one where lack of mobility isn't a thing and neither is fear about it.

This task might be a third alongside the other two, or it might just be the consequence of the other two. Again, it's a task any Church member should be encouraged to try. No matter who bumps into you and how and where, their depth is as precious as your own that you spend so much time praying about. Let us not become scary starers who gaze right into a person's soul on first meeting them; but let us treat everyone as having a lot more to them than meets the human eye, that's all.

Those, it seems to me, are among the key ingredients of the activity we call ministry, outward and inward, ceremonial and spiritual. In one denomination, it's believed they are expressed first and foremost in a sacramental ministry, with daily mass said by clergy and the visibility of a person's depth exposed in a practice of individual confession. In another tradition, nothing ranks above the commitment of practical love far beyond the worshipping congregation, and that is how every soul is given the dignity God means us to accord each other. One minister knows how to shape structures and processes to enable others to find their way of loving with God's love. Another is disarmingly impractical but creates a praying space around them wherever they go, and calms spirits all around. And, to be honest, some people minister without benefit of ordination, because in the most worldly of careers they treat unlikely and undeserving souls as utterly beloved. Others have ticked all the boxes of induction to a parish, convenership of an Assembly Committee, moderatorship of their Presbytery, and yet feel they are beginners in the practice of the presence of God, and with more to learn than to teach.

I have still to unpack the first part of my earlier phrase 'a sense of (1) being called (2) to do or be something'. What does the call look or sound or feel like?

I have never served as an assessor in the national process of selection that an applicant for training has to undergo. However, I have undergone a long-defunct prehistoric version of the process myself, and I have much more recently chaired the committee that runs it. So I have a small sense of what those decision-makers are looking to discern in those they will accept on the Church's behalf.

First, there needs to be a sense that the idea has come from beyond the individual and those around them, and must have come from God. This is fraught with difficulty. The Church will not thrive if its ministers are subject to mad hallucinations, so anything that sounds like a supernatural experience has to be weighed carefully to discriminate between calling and fantasy. In other applicants, though, the problem is perhaps the very opposite, because theirs is a very rational, naturalistic faith that doesn't experience visions or voices or anything like that; and those individuals famously struggle to describe anything external at all. The broad Church of Scotland does its best with an equally broad range of applicants.

Second, the assessment process does a little testing of the individual's ability to undergo formation, by setting some exercises for them to attempt: some are the kind of table-top fun tasks you may have encountered in other assessment processes (eg military, civil service), while others might involve doing a piece of writing about an imagined tricky parish situation. Again there is a danger in this; at a point before any formal training is begun, the Church is already looking for a skill-set, for someone with the fundamental characteristics that can be developed all the way to ordination and beyond. It is, I suppose, a corporate act of faith that God would not call someone who does not have even a potential for training.

A third sign that there is a calling lies in the applicant's sense of what their ministry might look like, and what gifts and graces they would bring to it. As those who apply to this process tend these days to have parts of their working lives behind them, the Church is being offered proven skills in management, IT, charity governance, teaching, counselling, and endless others. Is it a legitimate method of discerning vocation to recognise what a gift a particular life would bring into ministry? Is that a properly spiritual criterion to use?

There are certainly other areas of assessment used too. All of them judge whether the inner calling sensed by the individual correlates to a similar sense by the Church's representatives. Their question may meet with a painful answer, 'no', but one that probably spares one side or the other from damage and greater misery in the long-run. Sometimes it finds the wrong answer because the individual did whatever it took to give the answers that seemed to be 'right'.

In mid June 1986, I had reached the stage of the application process when I had to travel to Edinburgh from Kirkwall to undergo that residential assessment in St Colm's College in Inverleith (with its tiny beds perfect for the tiny deaconesses and missionary ladies who had trained there over the generations). One thing I am proud of from that nerve-wracking experience is that I resolved two things in advance, as I'm sure many people do: (1) that I would be ruthlessly honest in answering every question even if I felt as if I was damaging my chances of acceptance and then (2)

OH ALL RIGHT THEN

I would accept without hesitation whatever the result was, because I would know it was an assessment of the most real and honest version of me. Had I not been accepted for training on that occasion, I don't know if I would have gone back for a second or third attempt, as is normally possible. I am not recommending such a 'once only' attitude, however; I will never forget a fellow student who graciously accepted that she had thought things through after one non-accept, and when she was accepted a year later openly acknowledged that the earlier decision had, at that moment, been the right one for her and for the Church.

One thing does always make me suspicious, the applicant who paints herself as a most reluctant sinner being dragged by the Spirit kicking and resisting to the point of application, a martyr to a calling she cannot resist though she would love to be doing anything else. Too often those hystrionics seem to occur in someone who is very cross when they are told 'no', and who frankly seemed to be relishing the idea of being a minister in all sorts of ways they betrayed in their conversation from the outset.

So there is one more sign of calling, I would like to dare to suggest. If you think ministry would bring you happiness, satisfaction, fulfilment of your abilities and an expression of your faith that goes beyond anything else you can imagine, perhaps that is a God-given feeling, and not one you have to hide behind a grim mask. It is all right to think you might find joy in it.

Enough reflection on big questions for now. Let me take you back to the point half way in time between the cliff-top moment where we began and the tiddly little bed in the Ebenezer Room in St Colm's. The gate-keeper of access to national assessment was the local Presbytery, and in my case that was Orkney. I had to negotiate an interview with a committee of the Presbytery; and on this occasion it consisted of Bill Cant, the minister of St Magnus' Cathedral, along with another minister and an elder. Orcadian church folk above a certain age will remember the vestry of the Paterson Church, by then properly known as the East Church but only when people were minding their Ps and Qs. The church hall, then the meeting-place of the Presbytery as a whole, was the kind of slightly dusty Victorian space that served the Church for decades all over Scotland, furnished with the kind of chairs we were daft enough to think would entice anyone to want to be there at all.

Anyway, I had characteristically arrived way too early, and was sitting in the hall waiting to be called through to the grilling in the vestry. If I had known that when I got there Bill was going to ask me to describe my ontological and soteriological Christology I might have done a runner there and then. But if I had known that he would then go on and answer the question himself at length, I would have been able to relax again. The elder wandered through the hall, spotted me sitting there and no doubt sensed that I was a bit tense. 'Dinna worry,' he said. 'Yer gan ti be acceptit the night.' Never one to think before I speak, I remonstrated, 'How can you know that before you have interviewed me?' 'Ah weel, wir discovert that if wi accept you, will hiv mair candidates fur the ministry than Lewis Presbytery his got; and wir never had that afore.'

Graduating LLB, July 1984, with a headful of confusion

SERMON ON BEING CALLED: SAMUEL

In the first month of a new year, facing forward into the unknown, everyone wonders what challenges they'll have to face in the coming twelve months, what achievements they'll have to attempt as this year unfolds. Two weeks into January, with all the artificial silliness of the New Year celebrations fading in our minds and the resolutions we made there no longer novel or interesting, we're into the real thing.

Those of us who have a religious turn of mind have another way of thinking of those challenges ahead: we suspect that God may **call** us to do or be or try certain things, things of God's choosing not of ours, things that will suit God's purposes not our own fancy. Being called by God is not an idea we're comfortable with, unless we're fanatical about our spiritual experiences. To most of us it's a bit too spooky and weird to be comfortable; and the idea of God calling me, every 'me' will say, seems rather unlikely.

Today's lectionary readings each tell about God's calling, and each has something very easy to learn and remember.

1 Samuel 3:1-10

We wouldn't like it if God went speaking in the middle of the night to any small child we care about, in the way the Divine voice did to the boy Samuel. Across the centuries, as our way of being religious has changed and so has our way of raising children, so we have different expectations of God's care for our little ones. It's missing the point if this famous passage is only read and enjoyed as a picture of childish piety of an old-fashioned kind.

Eli the priest had a pair of shocking sons, and had done too little to bring them into line. Their behaviour was outrageous, sacrilegious and scandalous; and God could no longer use that house and family to be the point of contact with Israel. God needed to speak through someone completely new, fresh and unspoiled, someone with so little baggage that he would have to be heard and believed.

There's nothing impressive or holy about Samuel when he hears God's voice: he thinks it's the voice of Eli his master and runs to him. It's Eli who first recognises the voice of God going straight past him, by-passing him in favour of the young child. It's Eli who ensures Samuel listens properly for the message. It's Eli, later in the story than our reading, who hears God's condemnation of him and his sons and accepts that God's will must be done.

Let us who are tired and imperfect, and guilty that we don't really hear God's voice… and terribly relieved, really, when we don't… let us go about with open minds for the possibility that we may hear a pure and transforming truth in an unexpected place, from an unexpected direction. Let's accept that it's more important to be the ones doing God's will than it is to be the ones who happen to hear God's voice. Let's be willing to hear God in people whose appearance, or age, or lack of religion, or life-choices, make them seem unlikely prophets. But let's not avoid the responsibility by assuming that will always be somebody else. Each one of us in our prayers must admit: It could be me, Lord; what do I need to be saying and what do you need me to be making clear?

St John 1:43-end

This passage about Jesus seeing Nathanael under the tree is a bit of a mystery. There are clues. 'Nathanael' is a Hebrew word meaning 'God-given', and Jesus describes this person as a real Israelite. So Nathanael may be a description rather than a real name, which would make sense since none of the other Gospel-writers use that name for any of the disciples. We don't know which one this guy was. Then, if a Jew was asking what sort of a person someone was, he might use the phrase 'Under what tree is he?' Jesus had spotted Nathanael earlier on sitting under a fig tree, and that was regarded as a sign of someone who studied the Jewish law and was faithful to it. So Nathanael was a pure and faithful Israelite, a gift of God, someone made of the right stuff.

I don't think we have all the bits we need in this story – that is the kind of messy bundle the Bible is – but we have enough to know that Jesus had looked at Nathanael before Nathanael knew he was being watched, and Christ knew exactly what he needed to know, enough to choose and call him, enough to trust him.

We are such sophisticated and complicated beings towards each other, trying to keep our bit of mystery, our privacy. But that is not the way God sees us, sees right into us and knows us.

Psalm 139

We have a knee-jerk reaction against being known these days. The prospect of government-issued identity cards makes lots of people very cross, though few people have any particular details that ought not to be known. We live in a society in which two opposing pieces of legislation are constantly in conflict: Freedom of Information laws make us think we're entitled to have all the information we want about other people; while Data Protection laws make us think we should keep our own details private and resent other people knowing anything that might be useful to them. We're like primary school children with our elbows crooked round our spelling jotters, at one and the same moment terribly keen to see our neighbours' work but terribly keen they won't see ours. We live in a society that is no longer universally familiar with Psalm 139, a society that has lost its grasp of the promise that God knows us through and through, physically, emotionally, spiritually, socially, eternally – and being known like that is a cause for rejoicing, not a cause for resentment. What a relief it is to remember that my aches and pains, my fears and worries, my failures and ambitions, my loves and yearnings are completely known to God so that I am not ultimately alone with all of these things. What a relief it is to believe that God will never ask me to do more than I'm capable of doing because that same God knows better than I do myself what I'm able for. God may ask me to sacrifice my dignity, my reputation, my popularity, even my physical life in the service of the coming Kingdom of Christ. But God will always ask for what God knows I have to give.

Whatever God calls you to do and to be, spouse, parent, grand-parent, prophet, priest, pastor, neighbour, friend to the friendless, voice for the oppressed, charity-worker, elder, lover, carer: you are called because you are completely known and completely loved.

But there are things you and I will never be called to do.

Revelation 5:1-10

There are things you and I will never be called to do, because only Jesus Christ could do them. Some of them we are good at recognising. Only Jesus Christ could be born into this world as the Word of God made flesh, the incarnation of the promise of God to be with all people. Only Jesus Christ could show us what God is like by a life of perfect service and utter sacrifice. Only Jesus Christ could take our brokenness and fault, could take the skewedness of the whole world, take it through death and Hell and battle against the deepest of evil. Only Jesus Christ could emerge triumphant from a struggle too deep for any of us to put fully into words, and declare God's victory.

What we too, too often forget is that only Jesus Christ could open the seals that unleash the final judgement on the world. Only Jesus Christ can declare what he finds in each of our souls. And if the world has not yet reached that final cataclysmic point of judgement, then let us not imagine that it's a job for us in the here and now. We would only do it badly if we tried to act like God. We would only judge people to condemnation as if they couldn't be redeemed. We would only damn people for the wrong reasons and fail to understand them deeply enough to forgive them. We would only treat some human beings as if they were of less worth to us than the people we find attractive. We would only share the blessings of our world unfairly, so that other people and the planet we live on would suffer.

True piety, real holiness, knows deep down that we cannot do without Jesus Christ because there are some things in the history of creation that only He is pure enough to do. Without him we are nothing; without him we are just playing at being godly.

And so no one of us should be conceited because we feel called by God. We should not imagine that we know it all, that we can do it all, that we deserve it all. If you are called by God to any of the million loving tasks waiting to be done each day, that makes you no better a person. But when we respond to God's call we are – God willing – a little more faithful, a little more obedient, a little more useful.

2 FORMATION FOR MINISTRY

One Sunday during my probationary placement at Fairmilehead Church in Edinburgh, I was due to preach the sermon while my supervisor, Rev Murray Chalmers, conducted the rest of the service. By the Saturday night my cold had reached the point at which I knew I was not going to be able to read my sermon out loud the next morning; and it was really too late to expect Murray to prepare another one from scratch. But he, being a gentleman as well as the kindest and wisest of supervisors, offered simply to read my script with all due attribution the next day.

This was 1991, in the earliest days of Amstrad computers and the printers that went with them. And those printers used 'continuous' computer paper, the kind with micro-perforations separating the pages from each other and from the punched margins that fitted onto the printer's toothed guide-wheel. Is it all flooding back into the memories of readers of a certain age? Perhaps my head was befuddled by the cold; perhaps, even so, I *should have thought to split the script into its individual pages*.

I was well enough to attend the train-wreck, I mean service. Into the pulpit went lovely Murray, and commendably gave his oratorical 'all' to reading his probationer's best homiletic efforts. It was grand for the first page, and then he tried to turn to page two, and discovered that page two was attached to, and *below*, page one. All he could do was push page one up the pulpit's lectern to reveal the second page; which was sort of OK in a pulpit with a decent-sized lectern… but only until he got to the bottom of page two. As he pushed page two away from him to reveal page three, yes, page one started to work its way – visibly to the congregation and horrified probationer – down the front of the pulpit fall, like an enormous roll of escaping loo paper. And then, like something out of a Gerard Hoffnung song, there eventually came the point, in a six or seven page script, when the cascading pages *weighed more than the remaining bundle on the lectern*.

Ministerial formation consists of a mixture of study and practical training. I won't describe it in detail, nor even the mix of it. That's partly because it changes from time to time, and as I write some quite large changes are beginning to be debated. And it's partly because the system as constituted at any particular moment is experienced quite differently by candidates who arrive with very varied qualifications, and even more varied experience (of life, of work, and of the Church). Essentially though, a Church of Scotland candidate in my generation ended up with one of the most rigorous intellectual formations found in any denomination anywhere, and juggled that study with a battery of other requirements which included part-time placements both during and after their time at university.

Academic theological study covers a range of topics most of which readers will have accurately predicted: Biblical Studies, Theology (both in the sense of how our beliefs have developed [Dogmatics], and in the sense of how we defend them in debate with external agencies and other academic disciplines [Apologetics]), Church History, and those disciplines of Practical Theology and Ethics in which the academic and professional overlap and ministry becomes a reflective exercise long after graduation.

In days to come there may be a wider range of methods of study, and not all of them will include 'on-site' university education. I hope, though, that my description of the more traditional route I and my friends took will give a feel for the overall experience of becoming a theological thinker and – vitally, in parish terms – teacher.

Candidates arrive in college with attitude. They are students after all. No two have quite the same attitude, but the attitudes can be positioned along a spectrum. At one end of the spectrum would be the candidate who is thinking 'Bring it on, teach me things I don't know, transform me as you turn me into a minister, blow my mind and excite me with new concepts.' At the other end of the spectrum, I fear, is the candidate who is thinking – perhaps has been encouraged to think – 'I'm going to survive this, this place is not going to damage what I know to be true, I'll do whatever it takes to graduate because I must, but beneath it all I am not going to be corrupted by it.' And there are many students who occupy some point in between those ends, and wrestle with the old and new thoughts and ideas that wriggle together inside their heads like Jacob and Esau in the womb.

For obvious example, take Biblical Studies. Someone like me turns up having previously always looked at the verses of the Bible pretty much in isolation from each other, as I tried to figure out what they meant and how they applied to me. Also, I'd only ever read them in English. Then suddenly, someone shows me the historical and geographical context in which they were written, and torpedoes any idea that (1) the same person wrote the whole of a book, or (2) the order in which those books appear in my Bible is the order in which they were produced. With or without any formal study of Hebrew or Greek (it's possible to do the degree with or without), I learn about the language of the Bible, and find out that one word in the original has been translated using different ones in English, and that Aramaic colloquialisms cast dramatic new overtones onto words that had perhaps seemed lifeless before. I could go on and on. There are ministers who talk lovingly of embracing those new realisations, of loving the feeling of being reshaped by something that is probably a perfect example of the real meaning of 'education'. Be like them.

As I think back several decades to that mind-opening experience, I realise that I was being prepared to offer it to those I have served in a preaching ministry. What a privilege, and what a weighty responsibility that is. For me, there is great satisfaction in seeing a congregation realise that the Bible 'says' something they had never realised it 'said', or that its message is much more about the reality of their lives than they thought it could be. Suggest that St Paul was much more of a feminist than they've ever been told he was, and you'll have women ask if you'll let them take your printed sermon script home with them. Point out that a stricter translation of the Greek phrase normally rendered 'hardness of heart' would be 'cardiac sclerosis', and you're beginning to turn people's attention from their sin alone to their emotional fears, in a beautiful way that might unlock something in someone's own sclerotic heart.

Ministers probably replicate in their own congregations whichever of the attitudes they nursed in their own student days. You can teach people to discover much more by embracing the context and nuance of a verse; but you can also teach people to demonise contextual theology and base their own on the first-impression literal meaning of arbitrarily-privileged individual verses of a flawed old English translation. It's up to you; it's really up to you. So you have a very big decision of principle to make right from the off, and long before your ordination.

OH ALL RIGHT THEN

I would say one other thing about the study of theology, and hope I won't offend close friends in academic posts by this. Theological study is as difficult as you choose to make it. There are degree courses that are very difficult, even to achieve just the basic required standard (medicine and law spring to mind). There are, by contrast, technical subjects that may not require a particularly scholarly brain. Theology, in contrast to both of those sorts of courses, is a lot like many Arts subjects; the entrance requirements are not as high as they are for disciplines like medicine, and a reasonable level of application is sufficient to gain an ordinary degree and tick the particular subject-boxes the Church requires of you. You can do this even if you don't think you're a natural scholar, honest. If, though, you want to go further, to stretch a brain that happens to enjoy study, to become a specialist in a topic that has grabbed you when you first met it, to offer something unique to the Church from your own thinking (see Chapter 5), there is no upper limit to the possibilities. A cohort of Church candidates starting out together in a Scottish Divinity School will probably be intellectually diverse, and that of course is another source of stimulation for each of them.

Time for another story before I say something about the more practical aspects of the 'creation' of a new minister.

I've stressed that the practical elements of training vary from age to age, and back in my day we had space in our lives to serve as unordained locums during summer holidays, in places so desperate they would put up even with our inexperience and youthful gaucheness. And so after one year at New College I found myself on the Orkney island of Sanday for ten weeks, camping in the partially-furnished manse[4] and learning the rhythm of a preaching and pastoral ministry in miniature. What I couldn't do at my stage of training, please note, was (1) sacraments (baptism and communion) and (2) wedding services.

There was, though, a wedding in the diary right in the middle of my stint there; it would have to be conducted by Ian, the Interim Moderator of the charge who lived in the East Mainland of Orkney and visited Sanday when the need arose. This was long before the era of civil celebrants or, also please note, registered wedding venues. In the North Isles of Orkney in 1988, weddings happened in parish churches and were conducted by proper ministers, and that was that.

A storm blew up, and I mean a storm big enough to be commented on even by Orcadians. The planes were off. The ferries were off. The wedding day had arrived, but the Interim Moderator, the flowers and half the guests had not. Someone with a smallish boat was found who was willing to make the treacherous journey from Kirkwall Harbour to Sanday's Kettletoft Pier with all these necessities on board, and all I had to do (all? hah!) was pick up Ian from the boat in the little blue Fiesta (ministers all had little blue Fiestas in the late 80s, it was a thing), give him a cup of tea in the manse and get him to the church on time. So that was all right.

Until the phone rang and it was Ian's wife Helen ringing from home, who felt she should maybe mention to me that her husband was the most seasick-prone human being she had ever met, so she was not at all sure that he would be capable of standing up long enough to conduct a wedding,

---

[4] The thing I remember about the Lady Manse was instructive of the expectations people have of ministers. The congregation had obviously furnished the manse, and especially the kitchen, with great kindness but 'by committee'. Everyone had apparently brought what they thought a minister would most need. There were three china tea services and no frying pan. I bought the latter from the General Store at Kettletoft, left it behind when I left at the end of the summer, and visualised the conversation that would ensue as they tried in vain to work out whose it was...

or at least not without throwing up which wouldn't be a good look would it.

I knew enough about marriage law to know that I had just one other option. I asked an elder who the island's Registrar was, and phoned the number I was given. A friendly lady answered, and I explained to her my possible predicament. I could conduct a service of thanksgiving; I could even facilitate the taking of some kind of religious-not-legal vows and the exchanging of rings; but it was possible that I was going to need her to conduct a minimal form of civil marriage first. And if that was the case, the marriage schedule I had was going to be all wrong. No problem, said the friendly voice, she would produce a second schedule and we'd just use whichever one described the eventual outcome.

Then another thought struck the brain of the recently-qualified solicitor. The Registrar couldn't conduct the civil wedding in the church building, but only in her office. Where, might I ask, *was* her office? There was a bit of a pause, followed by 'I suppose I'd better hoover my sitting-room.'

Experiences like that one, in their terrifying way, help to form you for the adventures ahead. After that summer I knew that nothing that happened to me at a wedding would scare me ever again. Fortunately, though, the practical side of 'initial ministerial education' does have a more intentional and structured element too; and the biggest element of that comes in the form of the attachments that are served part-time during the degree, and full-time for a chunk of time between graduation and ordination.

You can think of these placements as attaching you to a **congregation**: you may experience a rhythm of weekday activity quite different from the routine of your home congregation, discover how varied liturgy can be within the range of legitimate Church of Scotland styles, observe the stresses and strains of working with difficult office-bearers, and of course try out your mad unpolished ideas on a new audience that will indulge you because you're a student for ministry and therefore by definition sweet and forgiveable.

I suspect, though, that most students will describe their experiences in terms of attachment to the supervising **minister**: observing everything from their theology to their diary-keeping, from their diplomatic skill level to their own devotional lives. Hours spent down-loading as much of the boss's experience into your own head as you can squeeze in there, debates between the self-evident truth of things you've just been taught in lectures and the rather more weathered wisdom your supervisor finds works for people, all of this starts to give you heft as a leader for the Church somewhere some day soon.

Some of our most influential ministers have achieved astonishing 'reach' across the Church simply because they have supervised so many ministers in training and influenced their styles.[5]

There are of course tips, tricks and urban myths in every generation of trainee ministers, the methods and stratagems used to get through all the elements of academic and practical training as painlessly as possible. In my day, one of the myths was that the training staff from 121 George Street[6] did not like to be told by a candidate where they should be sent for student attachments or probationary placement, but that by describing the place without naming it, you could nudge them in the right direction. I think that was total huey, but we believed it at the time.

An older student I admired had had a wonderful time at Colinton Church in South Edinburgh, and I thought it

---

[5] In Edinburgh alone you might think of Gilleasbuig Macmillan at St Giles, Bill Johnstone at Colinton, Murray Chalmers at Fairmilehead, and several other ministerial giants, all at the height of their influence when I was an ordinand.

[66] '121' is the standard term for the Church's central administrative offices. Whether it is used as a term of affection or abuse can generally be determined by context and tone of voice.

sounded like my kind of place. So when the formal conversation took place, I did my best to herd the minds of the decision-makers in exactly the right direction. I spoke of living on the south side of the centre of Edinburgh, and my hopes that I wouldn't have too much commuting to do. I spoke of my interest in a middle-class parish with lots of weekday activities, and a reputation for excellent pastoral care, and perhaps the financial resources to allow me to spend a little more than just the length of the probationary period there. I was well pleased with my efforts. And, quite reasonably, 121 sent me to Fairmilehead Church, two parishes to the right of Colinton on the map of South Edinburgh, but otherwise…. Of course, now I wouldn't have had it otherwise.

If the lasting influence of a supervisor can colour a future ministry or set a template of style in a preacher, then the relationships and connections formed back in college will provide a community of support within the wider community of the whole Church, one that will last far into the future. There are two parts to that community: the staff who teach you and the students who learn with you.

We mourn the passing of an age when many of the staff in those colleges were Church of Scotland ministers; now almost none are, even to the extent that the pastoral care of our ordinands occasionally has to be delivered from outwith the institutions. Probably it is true that the career-long connections are strongest with the staff who themselves have ordained experience and knowledge. Often, though, ministers draw strength and support from those whose kindness and sensitivity as teachers has most inspired them: many in my New College generation kept in touch with people like James Mackey and Noel O'Donoghue, the first Catholic staff to help to prepare Presbyterian candidates in Edinburgh. In Chapter Five I will say more about that long-term sense of belonging to our bit of 'the academy', and how we can pay something back.

OH ALL RIGHT THEN

And then there are the other students. They represent every type of denomination, every corner of the planet. every zany theological complexion. Sometimes they struggle with the things that make you struggle, and sometimes it is the things they find blindingly obvious that make you struggle in the first place. Within the cohort of CofS candidates there will be people you know will never invite you to occupy any pulpit they control in future (and that's fine with you), but you will pray for each other and help each other and take joy in each other's families and successes and dreams. And twenty years later, when you are wondering about applying for a parish in a part of the country you don't know, and the Year Book tells you that one of your group is in the same Presbytery, you will phone them up and take them into your confidence, and you will implicitly trust them when they say you shouldn't touch St Mungo's Up The Lum with a ten-foot pole, even though you never agreed with a theological word that crossed their lips back when you both had colour in your hair. You and they will know what you're on about when you recall the angels in the corner of room 66 whose appearance (only to Father Noel himself) would sometimes interrupt the flow of his explanation of 'Plato's theory of forms and its adoption in patristic theology' – and no-one who wasn't there would believe you for a second. You and they both find the concept of the 'wrath' of God even more terrifying than most people do, because the way Bruce MacCormick pronounced that word with his American accent in Systematic Theology 2B somehow made it worse.

So you'll seek out your peer-group for ever, visiting them on holiday, attending their churches when you're in the area, knowing that they understand the very shape of you because they were there when you were being constructed, lecture by lecture, essay by essay, Tunnock's Caramel Wafer by Tunnock's Caramel Wafer.[7]

I can't finish this little section without mentioning that our theological colleges are places of faith and worship. Of course that is a tricky area in a British university sector that has to be awfully careful about discrimination, inclusion and academic neutrality. The Church's presence – and I mean the Churches' presence (plural, not just CofS) – in our colleges enables a pattern of daily, weekly, termly prayer, services and sacramental life for those who surely need to keep spiritual formation foremost in the whole process. That is precious, in a place where your beliefs will be intellectually challenged and your faith will feel the punch sometimes. That is precious, when your early attempts to craft beautiful prayers are being heard by those friends who will be kind to you about them, and by lecturers whose advice you trust. That is precious, when the very candidates who can't believe you can possibly hold the beliefs you do… will be praying for you when you are ill or bereaved or failing your assignments. And they, as I think I've just suggested, will probably still be praying for you in 20 years' time.

If there are any current ministers reading this book[8], I think my question for our generation is how we approach the important task of being that older element of such a community, being the people whose ways are younger ministers' examples (God help them but it's true).[9] It is unsettling, in my early 60s, to clock that newer ministers are treating me the way I treated the experienced, well-known ministers a generation or two older than me in the 1980s and 90s. While my generation thinks we don't have the big

---

[7] Other theological institution may have had a different staple diet.

[8] Oddly, I have not written it for them, only about them. But if you're out there, colleagues, I'd love to see the marginal notes you're scribbling in approval or fury.

[9] My comments about involvement in the Church's intellectual life, in Chapter 5, provide part of the answer to that sort of question.

characters that used to stalk the Church, that we are insipid compared to them, no doubt there are students in the common rooms of our Divinity Schools today swapping awed stories of the crazy exploits of Glover or Gardner or Browning or MacLean. Eek.

This next story took place just days after my ordination service, strictly speaking after my formal training was over; but it involves New College so I shall close this chapter with it.

Some students at the College had established a new theological society for liberal-minded candidates and others, and were preparing for their first day-long conference on a Saturday in the summer term. Noticing that the date they had picked happened to be just a week or two after my ordination[10], they asked if I would close the conference by conducting Holy Communion for them, my first experience of presiding at the Sacrament; and I must say how lovely it was to be asked to do it there of all places.

New College is a very ecumenical place, full of thoughtful people who are attuned to each others' ecclesiastical sensitivities and practices. One of the manifestations of that kindness, in my era at least, was the practice of ensuring the consecrated bread was all consumed (ie Anglican-style), and not thrown away (as Presbyterians like me would normally do).

This fact was not at the front of my nervous head as I flapped about, getting ready to do this precious deed for the very first time. It was not until I had consecrated the small (but not that small), unsliced, brown loaf (I can see it yet, 33 years later), that I looked up and realised there were nine of us in the little chapel. Nine. Two full slices each were not going to get through this thing.

At the end of the service I did not attempt to eat the 90% of the loaf that remained (Presbyterians pinch off

---

[10] I was to stay at Fairmilehead for a further year as its ordained Assistant Minister, having completed my probationary period there.

astonishingly tiny pieces of bread, for some reason). I said to the organisers, with as much authority as I could muster, 'Be assured, this consecrated bread will be consumed by communicant members of Christ's Church today'.

About three hours later, my three male flatmates were watching football on the telly in our hallway, when they were a little surprised to be handed large bowlfuls of bread-and-butter pudding and custard, with the words 'Eat it all, every crumb; ask no questions'. I will neither confirm nor deny that one of them is now the Chaplain of a famous English Hospital, while another is a Bishop.

.

Fairmilehead Church, Edinburgh

ADDRESS AT A GRADUATION THANKSGIVING SERVICE ST ANDREWS UNIVERSITY 2008 (READING FROM PSALM 119)

When I agreed to preach the homily at today's service, I asked the chaplain's office to provide a list of the subjects graduating today, so that I could find their **common theme** and use it for this address. Back came the answer, and I won't bore you with all of it, but it included: economics, molecular sciences, international relations, chemistry, film studies, social anthropology, internet computer-science management (that was all one thing, I think), and philosophy.

And I thought, 'Gee, thanks a bunch'.

I wondered what common discipline could possibly apply to today's multi-coloured array of academic hoods, and that took my mind to some of the disciplines that are **not** studied in this university.

It's possible to graduate from St Andrews in things you can't study here. The Principal had to do a certain amount of crisis management some time ago when one of the better newspapers on its web-site gave us an unusually high ranking for our engineering faculty. [*Note to reader: There is no engineering faculty in St Andrews.*] Earnest parents were puzzled to be turned away before their offspring had so much as filled out a UCAS form. And yet, have a look at the regulations on academic dress in the graduation programme, where you will find that the Bachelor of Engineering degree at this university has its own hood, Peacock Blue silk or cloth bordered with white fur, to be exact. Honest.

This afternoon, the University awards two honorary doctorates of laws, another faculty we noticeably lack, but that – if you think about the reading we heard from Psalm 119 – is a discipline none of us can ignore and none of us can ever exhaust. God's Eternal Law is the very design of the world; and the Divine Law of our Christian faith has its close cousins in every system of belief around the world, where men and women long to know what is expected of them above all else, and what is the infinite call they are meant to spend their lives answering.

The Psalmist has the anxiety shared by everyone in this chapel who are not graduands, but who are here because they profoundly love, or have taught, or have supported, those who will graduate today. Like us, the Psalmist wanted to know how any young person choosing their direction in life can be sure of retaining purity. Purity is a word with a bad press: it is easily confused with virginity, excruciatingly dull piety, quietism or a failure to live all the most interesting bits there are to life. But truthfully purity has a lot more to do with unclutteredness of mind, integrity of speech and conduct, sheer simplicity and driven-ness of life-choices.

And the Psalmist proclaims that purity, the best and most worthy style of life, is found by meditating on the deepest, most eternal truths, the very laws of God, and listening there for the answers to the great questions you probably now find yourself facing.

One great question is, What will you **do**, now that you are graduating? It's the question you will most often be asked by kind people during today, on Sally's lawn or over lunch or at the garden party, and they want to know what will be the next line on your CV, the first job, the second degree, the world travel. But I am both a lawyer and a preacher, so I get to ask it more darkly: what will you **do**?

If your answer is that you will amass as much financial wealth as possible, you have not been listening to me. Manoeuvring yourself into a position where you are surrounded by lots of physical resources is not of itself an answer to the question, What will you do, what will you **actually** do? If anything you will make yourself vulnerable to questions about what good you did not do when you had the means. But wealth is only an attribute, not a quality, and people have been discovering that truth, usually years after the Church pointed it out to them, for as long as the Church has existed.

If your answer is that you will have a lovely family life and enrich the world that way, I will say God bless you. But will God also please preserve us from the fashionable confusion these days of family life with morality. Politicians and religious leaders think that their support of the nuclear family is some kind of moral end all by itself, when it is often nothing more than allowing people to be thoroughly selfish and telling them it's somehow OK as long as it's done at the level of the household and not the individual. I'm all right Jack, the very antithesis of every Gospel standard, is replaced nowadays by 'I and my spouse and children are all right Jack'. And that is more noble how, exactly?

If your answer is that you will excel professionally, I will admire your talent and wish you success, but I will wait to see whether you do the slightest good or ever deserve praise. Niccolo Machiavelli and Josef Stalin excelled in their area of talent, but you would not choose to be either of them today. Being brilliant is not the right sort of answer to the question, But what will you **do**?

The Psalmist, long before the birth of Christ, suggested focusing on God's self-expression, and giving your all to being part of the unfolding of that transforming history of the world. And when, centuries later, God's self-expression **was** Jesus Christ, nothing was left out in the process of making the whole world new. Into that transforming process were thrown birth, life, relationships, passion, energy, anger, heartbreak, death, heaven and hell. Responding to the great eternal noise of that drama and choosing to be part of it, listening for the words and Word of God and choosing radical obedience to that shocking purity of purpose, studying the law of God – the discipline from which no-one can ever graduate – and being driven by it to do things utterly beyond yourself: that is what you should **do**, actually **do**.

OH ALL RIGHT THEN

And today's the day you lose your best excuse for failing to do it. Until now you were off the hook, you were being educated, trained, formed, completed, prepared. Not any more. At the end of the graduation ceremony we will process out of the Younger Hall and you new graduates will process behind us as the newest members of the academic community, and as you emerge onto North Street you will leave behind all your excuses; and you will spend the rest of your life answering the question: But what will you do?

Thanks be to God, law-giver, life-giver, promise-giver. Amen

3 STROMNESS AND GRAEMSAY

A Sunday afternoon in the late 90s, and MV Graemsay bobbed her way across Hoy Sound from Stromness Harbour to the pier on the tiny island whose name she bears.[11]   Graemsay is one of the least populated of Orkneys's inhabited islands, with fewer than thirty people in total and rarely more than one or two primary-school-aged children. When the tiny school closed, its last pupil commuted on the boat each day to Stromness Primary School with a Council-supplied chaperone, and was surprised to find himself the subject of *News at Ten's* much-loved 'and finally' feature under the headline 'Is this Britain's loneliest schoolboy?'. Early in my tenure the little church – unsafe to use as such, with neither power nor water and too remote to acquire either – had been disposed of, and the island had become part of the parish area of Stromness. In that semi-detached way that always happens with a separate land mass in a single parish, the people need to be ministered to quite intentionally and not left to the

---

[11] Graemsay is still in service in 2024, looking a little like a child's bathtub tug-boat, serving the triangular route from Stromness round Graemsay to Moaness in North Hoy and home via the Graemsay Pier below the Hoy High lighthouse.

impossible task of making themselves part of a larger congregation they have no way of joining in any meaningful way.

So once a month on a Sunday afternoon, as the local minister, I would charter the ferry on behalf of the Church of Scotland, rustle up one or two people who fancied a very small adventure, and go to Graemsay for the afternoon. The school was still open in my time, so we met there for our service, and I would like to claim one of the best ratios of attendance to membership anywhere outside of the Western Isles. Four communicant members of the Stromness and Graemsay congregation lived in Graemsay; but with nothing else to do, the service and its accompanying refreshments were the best and only attraction at that point in a weekend, and so we would routinely have a dozen souls present – adults, children, babies.

I wonder if you would agree that there are two kinds of ecumenical co-operation: the 'push' kind and the 'pull' kind. By 'push' I mean the initiatives taken by churches locally or nationally to come together and work together, to choose to do things like united Holy Week services, or even to plan for the uniting of congregations and missions from the different traditions. By 'pull' I mean that something just happens because it has to, and no-one attaches the word 'ecumenical' to it until afterwards because that wasn't the motivation at the time.

The last head teacher in Graemsay was a Roman Catholic lady who pretty much ran the Church of Scotland there. She was the person with whom I would make the arrangements, she would prepare the school for us, and she would bring her guitar to accompany the hymns (with a gentlewomen's agreement that I wouldn't pick anything esoteric that wouldn't work with such an accompaniment, so we tended to stick like glue to *Junior Praise*). As well as being great fun, with a stock of stories mainly against herself, she was everything you would hope for in, say, the

OH ALL RIGHT THEN

Session Clerk of a small congregation. Off she would go during the week to Kirkwall for confession and mass, but did more for our denomination than most of its members are ever asked to do.

There we would sit in a circle, on the school chairs and surrounded by children's artwork, sharing a truncated version of the service I'd led four hours earlier in Stromness Kirk. Britain's loneliest schoolboy, I have to say, was the best taker-upper of an in-service offering I've ever met. Aged about six when I first knew him, he would take the velvet offering bag (you know the kind) and stand in front of each adult in turn, not moving on until he was satisfied with what he saw them putting into it. Every congregation needs him.

I have three chapters to write about my three spells in parish ministry that add up now to nearly twenty years. In this first one, I'll try to say something about a first solo ministry, and the theological 'fit' of minister and congregation.

Stromness, at first glance, looked like a wonderful charge for a recently-ordained minister. It was big enough to have a busy community and lots of people around, but small enough to get to know. Its printed parish profile implied that it was middle-of-the-road in terms of its style and doctrine, and it used conventional Church of Scotland hymnody. Let me go no further without saying that I had an extremely happy nearly-seven years in Stromness, and was very sad when the course of my developing ministry led me to feel I had to leave long before I was ready in my heart to say goodbye.

Stromness as a community is a most unexpected phenomenon, because it is a magnet for artists and intellectuals, a place of ideas and debate. That is partly because it was home to the poet/playwright/novelist George Mackay Brown, and a creative base for the composer Peter Maxwell Davies. The little town became rather a place of pilgrimage for their admirers, many of whom came to visit and never left – a common experience for innocent sojourners who fail to take sufficient account of the magnetic force of the place. To be the parish minister in a place like that required, still requires, the ability to operate over a big cultural bandwith, more so than in most otherwise similar-looking parishes.

And for a small place it has a complex religious character. Nowadays, it is a community with a varied offering of Christian worshipping communities, something to suit anyone's religious upbringing and preference, including small Episcopal and Grace Church congregations and a healthy Baptist Church. In the early 90s, apart from the largish CofS and very small Scottish Episcopal congregations, and a small group meeting in a house for mass, there was a very tiny Brethren Group and an Orkney-wide independent fellowship that met in the secondary school a mile away on the other side of the harbour, but no Baptist or similar presence in the heart of the town. And that meant that there was a much trickier kind of bandwidth – theological this time – of people trying to operate all together *within the parish church*.

This was, of course, my first inducted ministry, and I had come from a home background, various training placements, and the delightful period at Fairmilehead, which were all quite cohesive communities with shared expectations and priorities. Not so much Stromness. Within the congregation, no liberal or moderate minister was going to meet the needs of some of the congregation, and I'm not sure there's much in our training about riding a chariot that has two horses pulling in different directions.

I'm sure that in my newly-trained innocence I thought I ought to try to keep these people all together 'inside the one tent'. Looking back at a few scripts and sermons that survive as the archaeological artefacts of that first ministry, I can see that I patently failed those at one end of the theological spectrum; I just could not in conscience betray the kind of liberal, poetic, ecumenical, permissive principles that bear the weight of my understanding of our faith. The office-bearers and members who came out of a very different tradition were obviously unhappy with my ministry, and I was young enough and eager enough to please that I was sometimes pretty unhappy with their unhappiness. At the time I didn't really have a way of measuring that; so, as I said earlier and I mean it, I felt very happy *overall* while I was there. It was later, in other ministries, when the congregations were more like the ones I'd known before, and when I had the advantage of increasing age and poise, that I looked back and realised I'd had some tough moments in those early years.

One of the greatest gifts I ever received, therefore, was a friendship with two people there whose job was to remind me from time to time that it 'wasn't me', to provide an external arbitration of whether I was over-reacting or just putting up with criticism that should not push me off my path. When you can find a couple whose support of a young single minister extends to nursing her after the removal of her wisdom teeth, to the extent of pushing mashed banana down her throat when she can't consume anything else or move her jaws at all for a day or two, you know God is looking after you. When you realise you can consult their wisdom when it's your own foolish reactions you need to confess and not anything done by anyone else, you learn a great deal about grace (your own, actually, not just your mentors'). And when those angel-like friends are held in such high regard by the community that your friendship with them gives you credibility and the benefit of what otherwise might be considerable doubt, golly you have won a lottery somewhere.

I hope you read this as a narrative about a ministry, and not one about a congregation. Let me complete the story of the congregation though, to be fair to them. After me, they had more of the same in the next ministry, until the point at which something had to give and a new Baptist congregation was founded in the town centre. What a relief that must have been for those whose needs had not been met in at least ten years; and the parish church congregation became smaller, but I believe more at ease with itself, over quite a short time. The bits of inner debate that could hurt were no longer needed. I take equal pleasure in the greater happiness of those who left as I do for the congregation that remained. Today they face new challenges, relating to buildings and demographics; they will bring to those new questions their grace and open-mindedness, and they will do so as a community that coheres.

A wee story to give your brain a break before I reflect a bit on first-parish ministry.

Remember the 90s, and its mobile phones, and especially its mobile phone signal, and especially the mobile phone signal in Stromness if you know that slopey, nook-and-cranny-filled town that must be any signaller's nightmare?

One morning, on a day when the afternoon's task was a church funeral, I had cause to pop into the building for something, and noticed that the funeral director had already placed the coffin in front of the communion table. Now I'm not normally the type to feel supernatural presence, but standing there in that old United Presbyterian-style church with its horseshoe gallery shading the seats beneath, I just felt as if I was not alone. I glanced at the coffin, told myself not to be silly, glanced again, imagined I could hear something, somewhere, imagined even that there was a shadow falling over me.

You bet there was. Standing *on* the very highest pew in the gallery, blocking the light that should have been streaming in the east-facing window, and waving his mobile brick frantically to try to get a signal in the most elevated possible position, was the funeral director.

OH ALL RIGHT THEN

Back to the business in hand; what advice would I have for a first-time parish minister? The training our denomination gives to its clergy is more thorough than most and often held up as an example to other churches. Our clergy have a reputation for being intellectually robust, capable of handling a great deal of work, and good at creating social capital in their local communities. Much of that comes from what's known as our 'initial ministerial education'. In any profession though, there is much more to be learned that can't be noticed and absorbed – and even, sometimes, believed – until the individual practitioner is plunged into it for real with no training wheels attached.

The first thing people sometimes wonder about a first ministry is whether it is still the case that the convention is to have a short ministry to begin with in order to get the rookie mistakes out of your system, and then go somewhere bigger for a longer ministry amongst people who didn't see the early howlers and therefore might hold you in a bit more respect. And if it is still the convention, should it be?

It can't be in quite the way it was in my youth, simply because the length of ministries is greatly reduced by the advanced age at which most ministers now arrive at ordination. There is just no time in a fifteen year ministry to do five years in one place and then twenty in another. And with our newbie ministers being so much more mature and experienced in other careers than my generation was, they probably blunder a lot less too, and so there is less need for that test-bed style of first job.

As I think of my contemporaries in ministry, my mind goes to two in particular who, even in this modern age, have had the kind of very long single-ministry career that was much more common several generations ago; and in each case they have suffered no disadvantage in ignoring that convention.

Maybe what I want to say is not a comment about the length of the first ministry but about its content. That finding of style, experimenting with things half of which will flop and so may you, encountering situations for the first time and not always being able to stop and consult someone with more experience, all must be braved. Maybe, then, a first ministry should be tackled with flair and courage, and therefore with the attitude that it might not be a long one; and if it turns out that it is, you are blessed indeed (or just better at this stuff than most of us are).

The second thing I'd suggest is not to arrive with a plan. Being presbyterian, we don't suffer as much as more priestly denominations do from the phenomenon known as 'Father knows best', where it's assumed the clergy are beneficent dictators who get to decide everything. However we do sometimes make the mistake of thinking that we have an understanding of the needs of the church that must be better informed than the understanding of the laity we are going to serve and support. We make that mistake because we do not yet know them, and we do not yet know their situation. The grand theological plan for the transformation of worship may founder on the range of musical resources; the ambitious dream of buildings refurbishment may have to take a back seat to a leaky hall roof; the determination to blow revival through a moribund worshipping community may have been tried by a recent predecessor who had no diplomatic skills, and you will just scare them all off if you seem to be trying the same stunt too soon.

Rather, learn what unique things your congregation does, and then get yourself invited to be part of those. Discover the things you assumed were needed which in fact turn out to be unnecessary; discover things your wildest dreams had not presented to you which are oddly wonderful. Arrive without a cookie-cutter in your briefcase.

The third thing is the thing in which I most miserably failed back then, and it has taken me more than thirty years to feel I've even slightly corrected it. It is unqualifiedly *critical* to create space for three things: work-related reading, prayer, and time-management. There is every chance that you will love one of those and neglect either or both of the others. I'm a sucker for time-management tricks, and would spend ages working out a study-plan before my exams and have to steel myself to start actually following it.

What of prayer? The Church has developed in recent years a palette of resources to help ministers, including Ministerial Development Conversations, mentoring, learning materials for continuing development, and so on. The poor relation has been Spiritual Direction, and I shall commend that again towards the end of the book.

What of reading? The impertinent aphorism has an edge of truth in it, that you can guess the year of a minister's ordination by looking at their bookshelves; while there will be volumes from recent years there, those will be fewer and further between than the tomes from their honours subjects, and in some cases the signs will be that intellectual exercise has largely dried up or been swamped by all the urgent tasks that push scholarship to the back of the priority list.

And, finally, what of that organising of the gift of time? It is easy to lose one's mastery of one's diary early in ministry, when no preparation was made for the first wave of unusual busy-ness, and the in-tray (nowadays probably an electronic inbox) just never recovers. One of the casualties is likely to be the ability to measure one's own workload, which in turn leads to far too much agreeability to new tasks requested by other people.

The challenge, then, is to exercise the spirit, the mind and the energy-bank as diligently as you should your muscles or your digestive system.

But I'm sure there is no better way to learn this stuff than to learn from other people's unpredictable experiences, those ones no-one in college dreamed they should prepare you to negotiate.

OH ALL RIGHT THEN

Here is an example of the second item in the discussion above (don't arrive with a plan), of discovering the unexpected and unique riches of your first congregation, and of going with that flow with a wide open heart – and perhaps a healthy capacity to cope with the bizarre.

There lived in Stromness for many years a musical alchemist called Jean. She had taught locally, and in retirement continued to exert a magic spell on the children of Stromness and the wider West Mainland of Orkney, producing in them so much music that it flows to this day right through that rich cultural landscape. If she announced a concert of Scottish fiddle music, you could expect dozens and dozens of very small children playing very small fiddles, some managing the tune and others perhaps playing a drone-note on a open string but still having the thrill of performing. If you tried to visit her at home, she would invariably have another non-paying piano pupil just about to arrive. And in Church she and others led a Junior Praise Band. There was no Senior Praise Band, so I suppose they might easily have made a power-grab and just called it *the* Praise Band, but hey perhaps they lived in hope that the children would inspire some adults to pick up a guitar.

The deal, in my time, was this. The first hymn in the service would be one of the great classic hymns of the Church – *Holy, holy, holy* or *The Church's one foundation* or *Now thank we all our God,* that sort of thing – for the children present to learn by osmosis and carry with them in their musical and religious instincts for the rest of their lives. The second hymn, before the children left for Sunday School, would be led by the band, and they were given a lot of leeway to choose something appropriate for the point in the liturgical year, and I would be fairly relaxed if it was something I might not have chosen, or possibly didn't even know. And it was perfectly legitimate for Jean to apply some musical flexibility to use a better-known tune to fit existing words. So far so fair.

OH ALL RIGHT THEN

What happened on Good Friday in my second or third year there is almost wasted on printed text and I wish I had a recording of it for you to play; but you'll just have to imagine it. The hymn was *There is a green hill*, to which you'll agree there are not many different tunes used, and I drew breath to begin singing the tune I'm sure is in your head right now as you read this. But the introduction was completely different, certainly not a hymn tune I'd ever heard before, and yet, and yet, there was something curiously familiar about it, something just beyond the tip of my tongue to name but I just knew how the melody was going to unfold. And then, just before I had to sing the first line, I knew what it was. We were singing that great Good Friday text to the tune of the chorus of the Animals' *The house of the rising sun*. I can hear you trying it; it works though, doesn't it? So, which interpretation do you think sits worse with its Christian appropriation: that the house was a brothel (in the original Baez/Dylan versions), or that it was a casino (the version recorded by The Animals and subsequently The Doors)? Hmmm – it's an extreme twist on the early Reformation practice of setting psalm words to folk tunes, isn't it?

By the end of my ministry there, I looked forward to 'our' version of the hymn, and thought the tune interpreted the words very pointedly. To this day when I encounter *There is a…*, I think of that tune, those children, that very unshockable congregation, and I give thanks.

And finally…

Just before I started writing this book, the Church lost a senior former Moderator, Very Rev Dr Hugh Wyllie, and Mrs Wyllie, only a few weeks apart from each other. This is my favourite memory of them.

Hugh's moderatorial visits included one to the Presbytery of Orkney, and he thoughtfully asked that he would preach in the congregation of the newest minister. On the Wyllies' arrival at Stromness Church, one elder brought him through to find me in the vestry while another gathered up Mrs Wyllie, who by her behatted appearance could not have been anything other than the Moderator's lady, she really couldn't, really really. For some reason unknown to me, and in a moment of madness I can never now undo, the elder slotted Mrs W into the naughty pew. The naughty pew (about a quarter of the way back on the north side of the church, the congregation knows whom I mean) contained the kind of people who would leave a pan drop on the minister's lectern before the service just to see what would happen; though, to be fair, at least they didn't do *that* on that day.

But also in the naughty pew was a lady who went with life's flow. Over a couple of neighbours she leaned, to offer one of the aforementioned pan-drops to the unexpected visitor in her midst. Mrs Wyllie politely declined; she obviously wasn't an eater during worship – fair enough, each to their own. But her would-be hostess persisted, leaning over the others again to deliver the stage whisper, 'You'd better take one; it's not Miss MacLean today, it's some other man and he might go on for a while.'

A few months later, in his next Presbytery visit to Angus, Hugh asked this time to meet any recently-ordained elders at a reception. My mother[12] was waiting in the presentation line, and when introduced to the Moderator said, 'I believe you have met my daughter.' Hugh looked as if he hoped he would manage to remember whatever name he was about to be given, and when Mother said mine he burst out,

---

[12] Freda MacLean and the eldership of the Church of Scotland were not a match made in Heaven; the marriage did not last very long. It ended with an uncharacteristic vision of God, most definitely not my late mother's style. It was during a particularly 'formal' formal communion, the kind that has just a bit too much military-like precision and instruction and angst about detail. I will neither confirm nor deny that she referred to those sometimes as 'heel-clicking' Communions. On this occasion she suddenly imagined God leaning over a cloud, watching what was happening in the church below, and asking St Peter, 'What are these people doing?' And so she tendered her resignation. Readers who knew her will be smiling in recognition of the character.

OH ALL RIGHT THEN

'Marjory MacLean? Oh yes, I most certainly know her!' I've always thought he wasn't saying that in a *good* way, at the time...

On the terrace, Stromness Manse, 1992

SERMON
(READING: THE BEATITUDES)

I wonder whether Jesus really spoke all the Beatitudes in one go, or whether they are a collection of his blessings that were originally spoken one by one on different occasions, so that each one could be savoured and absorbed and brought to life.

I wonder whether a preacher who preached on nothing but these verses for a year would ever run out of things to say, or instead would find the blessing just extending further and further from those original words like pond-ripples.

So here are some Beatitudes for people like us in times like ours. There are quite a lot of them; so choose the one that most sounds as if it is for you, and take it with you from here.

"Blessed are the poor in spirit, for theirs is the kingdom of heaven.
God bless you if you are one of those people who thinks they are less important than other people, or if you somehow think you have done something to deserve your suffering, or if you have lost the will to try to live your best and fullest life. Christ sees you there in your too-small corner, and invites you to imagine yourself walking in a peaceful place, the size of a whole kingdom, where no-one is more dignified or important than you, and your spirit turns out to be as big and strong and rich as anyone else's. Walk in this life as if you are already in that place, for indeed you already have that dignity that no-one can strip away from you

Blessed are those who mourn, for they will be comforted.
God bless you if years and years ago you suffered a loss you could not imagine surviving, and the world is still looking grey instead of bright-coloured, and the edge of

someone's odour from a rarely-opened wardrobe still catches the back of your throat, and the contours of your innermost self seem to be defined by that lost person's absence and not by your own presence. The everlasting arms of Jesus, that seem a little cheesy when we sing about them, hold you in place like a baby cradled into an adult's neck; not to take away your grief – you daren't lose it or you might lose the memory of love that causes you to grieve – but you will be kept safe and find your strength in that. Let yourself feel as comforted as that even in a life that wobbles a bit sometimes.

Blessed are the meek, for they will inherit the earth.

God bless you if you are the person who keeps their own counsel when other people are arguing over each other's voices, who waits (without recognising it yourself) for your wisdom to be recognised at last by those who only think they are wise, who reckons you have blessing enough and never go chasing after new treasures. It is quiet people everywhere who are really the owners of the Earth after all, they are the ones who are still there tending and appreciating what is right there in front of them when power and greed has long since moved on. Keep being you, keep doing you, and in your fingers and in your breath the Holy Spirit will sneak onto the scene.

Blessed are those who hunger and thirst for righteousness, for they will be filled.

God bless you if your desire is to feed your soul, your spirit and your mind, and not just stuff your body and entertain your senses; if your desire for your grand-children is to propagate wisdom within them rather than surround them with wealth; if your concern for your community is as much about the elements that cannot be seen with the eyes as with the resources that can be; if you are unsatisfied with the world as it is because you suspect God is unsatisfied with the world as it is. You will always have a soul that feels as if it has just been filled with the loveliest meal; and when you pray, you will always give thanks more than you ask for help. Attend, then, to the inside of things and people and moments, and keep listening impatiently.

Blessed are the merciful, for they will receive mercy.

God bless you if you refuse to treat people as they deserve; if you give hospitality to the ungrateful, if you trust those who are likely to abuse trust, if you make space in your social circles for those who are at the most fragile stage of recovery from addiction, if you keep within the safety of your family circle someone who has behaved outrageously, if you exclude no-one from the warmth of welcome of your congregation. Christ does as much and more for the broken and corrupt bits of the middle of you, the bits of you that other people can't cope with and the bits other people have never discovered, thank goodness. Don't ever start measuring, or measuring out, justice; just keep crying out for those who need it.

Blessed are the pure in heart, for they will see God.

God bless you if you keep things simple in your thoughts, your prayers, your desires, your ambitions, your loves; if you resist the temptation to scheme or manipulate or conspire, or to imagine that others are scheming or manipulating or conspiring against you; if you look into the future and ask only to be good and faithful. You will find God in a thousand things and people, which you have been looking at for a long time perhaps without finding in them the face of the divine; and you will know you are facing in the right direction, and learn to keep your invisible depths uncluttered. Choose one thing to ask of God, and keep asking.

Blessed are the peacemakers, for they will be called children of God.

God bless you because you made peace between warring parties and you were one of the warring parties; and you had to eat humble pie or accept a blame you had not really earned; or when one of those at war was someone who always relies on you to be loyal to them whether they are right or not, and so you had to speak a difficult truth to them to pull them back from destruction; or when the war was really a physical battle and you had to do something rather brave to protect someone rather weak or small. Christ recognises in you the courage of body or conscience that drove him all the way through life and death and new life, and so he calls you God's child. Be the person others expect to bring new peace to any moment of theirs.

Blessed are those who are persecuted for righteousness' sake, for theirs is the kingdom of heaven. Blessed are you when people revile you and persecute you and utter all kinds of evil against you falsely on my account. Rejoice and be glad, for your reward is great in heaven, for in the same way they persecuted the prophets who were before you.

God bless you when you do not wallow in the false martyrdom of being resentful when you are asked to do something unglamorous for your family or workplace or church; but when you give your enemies a worthwhile reason to hate your guts by calling out selfishness or aggression or arbitrary cruelty. The Holy Spirit rejoices that sometimes you're up for being the mouthpiece of goodness and decency, no matter what it takes; and you will receive all that you could ever wish because your desires are the desires of God. Learn the strange economy of blessing and suffering that marks us out from all others, as adventurers who ensure all for the greatest cause.

Each of these is a blessing, not a prize. Each of these is something most people would heartily avoid, in order to live the kind of life our western world admires and most of the population emulates. Each of these assumes that you are fundamentally located in a place that belongs to God, and each of these assumes that your desires belong first and foremost in that place. Each of these blessings recalls that you have been blessed already, and that by your response you will be blessed more deeply with the same thing. Each of these blessings says nothing about any of the measures of success you might ordinarily calibrate: and those are not only money, fame or admiration, but they might be control over life-choices, discrimination in friendships, deciding what things make you angry or joyful – all of these might be sacrificed too.

And each of these blessings promises that you will offer everything and receive more than you give, and only you will know it.

EXCURSUS

Here's a bit of routine that probably intrigues Church members who have never had to do it: how to prepare a Sunday service? How long does it take, and in what order do you do all the bits, and to what extent can you cheat?

I'd like to suggest a formula for the amount of time it takes:

9a(100-b)%

- where 'a' is a personal variable (probably anywhere between 1.0 and 2.0) representing the number of hours it takes an experienced minister to construct an Order of Service, *or* invent a children's address, *or* compose prayers, with the writing of the sermon taking as long as everything else put together (giving a total of 6 x a)

- where 9a represents the fact that new ministers probably take half as long again as old ones to do any of these tasks (so it's 6a x 1.5)

- and where 'b' represents the exact number of years you have been a minister, to provide a smoothly sliding scale

Every minister reading this book has just done the sum for themselves, and one or two might even recognise themselves in it. The lightning fast newly ordained minister who can do any of these tasks in an hour is going to need about nine hours in total [9 x 1.0 x (100-0)/100 = 9], but once they have been ordained as long as I have it should reduce to 6 [9 x 1.0 x (100-33.3)/100 = 6] The easily-distracted old tortoise who was ordained in the same year as me and takes two hours just to get one of these jobs done will need twelve hours now [9 x 2.0 x (100-33.3)/100 = 12], having struggled away for almost half the week on their service when they were brand new [9 x 2.0 x (100-0)/100 = 18]

Well, something like that.

The order in which I've always done the bits is:

- Look at the lectionary readings for the relevant Sunday, mull them over, decide what the theme is

OH ALL RIGHT THEN

- and then construct the Order of Service. It may seem odd to do this first, but your organist will love you to give them this so early in the week.
- Write the sermon (possibly over two periods of time)
- Do everything else.

That means that on four part-mornings in the week I'm working towards Sunday's worship. As I tend to work in very intense bursts of energy, and am old and wily, I'm about a 6 on the algebra above.

Cheating also speeds up prep over the years, through use of what's known as 'the barrel', the growing stash of sermons which, with care, can be recycled to save lots of time. People who sneer at this practice on grounds of needing to be fresh and relevant and contemporary are unlucky: they must preach sermons so based in current events that they can't easily be re-used. A timeless sermon with a couple of contextualised illustrations, on the other hand, can be adapted with fresh examples that require the alteration of 20% of the text, taking '0.5a' of time (as defined above) to make new.

I cannot overstate my admiration for people who have their entire ministry in the same charge, *because they probably can't ever dip into their barrel,* and so they frankly make their own lives so much more difficult.

The file-names for my sermons also have a formula (why doesn't that surprise you any more than it does me?). An imaginary example might be: S-171202-K+A-BAdv1-Mk13-H2023, which would tell me that this was a Sermon first written for Kinnaird and Abernyte churches' service on Sunday 2 December 2017 (which was the first Sunday of Advent in Year B of the three-year lectionary). I was focussing on the Gospel reading which is from Mark chapter 13 on that Sunday of the cycle, and I rehashed it to use in 'the Hope' (as the village I now live in is known) six years later.

4 121 AND THE GENERAL ASSEMBLY

Once upon a time, the General Assembly of the Church of Scotland agreed to move out of its Assembly Hall to accommodate the fledgling Scottish Parliament. Actually it was twice upon a time, in 1999 and 2001, and it was on the second of these occasions that the Church ever so slightly altered its sacramental practice without reference to its theological experts.

The thing was: we were in Edinburgh's Usher Hall, which has stalls, a grand circle and a very high, very steeply-raked upper circle. Members of the Assembly were going to use the lower two levels, so members of the public would have to cope with the dizzying heights of 'the gods'. And that was fine, except for the General Assembly communion service, in which we are assiduous about including the public gallery in the distribution of the elements.

Communion is distributed in the Assembly by elders chosen from amongst the commissioners, and the selection we had represented a range of physical abilities. Not all of them were going to be confident taking a patten of bread or a full chalice all the way to the top of the building, and then step their way down the very steep steps from row to row with their hands still occupied.

OH ALL RIGHT THEN

This, therefore, was the year when the Assembly's Youth Representatives became communion stewards. That's not the liturgical innovation – you have never needed to be an elder to do that, whatever most congregational practice may be. No, the little bit of sacramentological tweaking was that the elements for consumption by members of the public sat on tables in the corridors behind the upper circle, and were deemed to have been consecrated at a distance from the Moderator who was standing in front of the stage. No-one seems to have been hurt in the process.

In a presbyterian type of Church, with no bishops or other bearers of individual authority like that, the national life of the whole Church, and the equipping and supervising of its regional and local parts, belongs to the sovereign body which we call the General Assembly. The Assembly itself meets for six days in late May each year in Edinburgh, and its membership of several hundred people includes ministers, elders and deacons (all on a rota), as well as many helpful non-voting members from other denominations, other countries, and other constituencies within our own ranks (young people, representatives from the committees I shall describe below, and so on).

The Assembly has quite a few functions. For legal purposes it is the rule-making 'parliament' of the Church, the place of accountability for its own executive functions, and the source of authority for appellate judicial functions (which it used to exercise itself, but now places in the hands of more expert bodies to do the work more thoroughly and much more discreetly). For constitutional purposes it is the place where the relationship of Church and State is expressed most visibly and elegantly, through the presence of the Lord High Commissioner. And in sheer religious terms, it is a crucible for celebratory worship, promotion of the work of agencies, equipping of mission through the sale of resources, and much more.

OH ALL RIGHT THEN

Most of those functions, you will realise, need to continue throughout the year between the end of one Assembly and the beginning of the next. And so there is an executive staff, based largely in 121 George Street (and, as we've already seen, collectively known as '121'), who carry those threads of activity through the year. They ensure instructions from the Assembly are implemented; they react to situations in which the Church has an interest; they do everything from running care homes to recruiting trainee ministers, from ensuring congregations are OSCR[13]-compliant in their accounting to engaging with the secular press when the Church finds itself in the news for good or ill. They do, actually, a thousand other things too.

And within 121 there are two types of role a minister might play. One is as a staff member, probably at managerial level, within one of the departments and agencies that do all this work. Normally this involves leaving parish ministry and instead becoming an employee of those central agencies; it is still very much a ministry – you might say it is ministering to those who minister – but it may allow the exercise of skills learned in a previous life before ordination which might otherwise be rather lost.

The second role that ministers (and others) play is as voting members of any of the many committees (using that term as a generality for things that might also be called Leadership Team, Panel, Trust, depending on their role). Every year the General Assembly appoints new members to all sorts of bodies, and looks for nominations. In a later chapter I shall tell a little of what that has felt like.

It was in the first kind of role that I spent the middle third of my ministry to date, serving from 1996 to 2010 as Depute Clerk of the General Assembly. That role began as a part-time appointment exercised alongside my ministry in Stromness, but in 1998 it became full-time and required me to move back to Edinburgh once again. As I said earlier, I

---

[13] The Office of the Scottish Charity Regulator

was sorry to leave Stromness, but knew I had to if I was ever going to have such an opportunity to use my prior professional training for the good of the Church.

Mind you, I did wonder just how it served the Kingdom when I worked for a day (uncredited, sadly) as wardrobe consultant on an episode of STV's Rebus mysteries, *The First Stone*, set in the General Assembly of the Church of Scotland where the Moderator-elect got bumped off, naked. The interiors were filmed in Edinburgh University's MacEwan Hall (spoiler: it was to allow for a denuement that involved someone falling from a high gallery – if you graduated in there you'll know it was perfect, once some very bouncy airbags had been installed). Down in the basement where generations of graduands have picked up their hired gowns and hoods, the extras were all costumed up, and my job was to check that the 'former Moderators' looked the part. There was a bit of a crazy mix of appearances, dress, age, gender, tidiness... Yup, I reckoned it was all pretty authentic and didn't correct much.

Seriously though, thinking of the range of jobs ministers do in 121, it really is an amazingly varied spread of specialities. One might be co-ordinating the extremely confidential and delicate process of the National Assessment conferences for those being assessed for ministerial training. Another might be planning an overseas trip for the incoming Moderator of the Assembly who has been asked to visit a country that will greatly benefit from very carefully-judged press coverage of such a tour. Another will have dozens of meetings each month with opposite numbers in friendly Scottish denominations to work together in local projects and on national issues of common concern. And then too those thousand other things.

OH ALL RIGHT THEN

And in the office of the Principal Clerk of the General Assembly, the Clerks and their colleagues will be drafting legislation for the next Assembly to consider, staffing a complicated range of internal judicial processes alongside the solicitors in the Law Department, wrestling with the vast complexity of running an event as long and diverse as the Assembly itself, and providing advice – sometimes required with great urgency – from people all over the Church who fear they may have got themselves into a procedural pickle or a knotty dispute or an embarrassing mess, who need to know how to navigate their way back to safety within the constraints of the Church's own rules.

A minister from the *very, very* far west phoned me at 121 one day for a bit of advice about a sticky procedural point; to be honest I can't remember what the problem was, but I will never forget how grateful he was when I suggested how he might proceed to deal with it. A token of his gratitude, he said, was on its way to me. If he is reading this, I hope it won't hurt his feelings too much to say I can't stand black pudding, not even Macleod of Stornoway black pudding. And deep in my heart I knew, I *knew* that's what it was going to be.

In an earlier story I spoke of that feeling when you can't see anyone but somehow sense that you are not alone. A few days after that phone call I had a similar experience. My PA Linda, who sat at a desk in our outer office just out of my sight but whom I could normally hear typing away or taking phone calls, suddenly went very quiet, so quiet she seemed hardly to be breathing. Through I went, the concerned kindly boss, and this is what I saw: Linda, still sitting on her chair which she had pushed as far back from her desk as she could, rigid like a statue; and amidst the pile of today's post on her desk a brown, paper, bomb-shaped parcel. 'It's all right,' I said quietly, 'I know what that is and it's not what you fear.'

OH ALL RIGHT THEN

I couldn't persuade Linda to take the thing home; I think she was still focusing on her heart rate. So I headed down to the café lounge and found John, who at the time was one of the mainstays of 121, working both in the café and as a cleaner in our offices. I did a deal with him; he cut the bomb into half a dozen thick slices, kept one for himself, cling-film-wrapped the others and gave them back to me in a poly bag. I wandered back up to my office with as many detours as it took to hand out slices of black pudding to those with better taste than mine – I seem to remember they were all men. Reverend Sir in the Western Isles, please forgive me and know you made far more people happy than you ever intended.

Imagine a cone pointing upwards. At that narrower, upper end imagine you have the Assembly, represented for most of the year by '121'. Half way down the cone you have the Presbyteries, nowadays about a dozen with probably a total membership of a couple of thousand people, I suppose. They help in that process of implementing policy and supervising local Churches, themselves subject to the Assembly but with some authority over congregations. At the broad end of the cone come congregations with their Kirk Sessions, the places most of us do most of our work for the Church.

You might be imagining a broad and shallow cone, six inches wide but only an inch high. Or you might be imagining something proportioned like an inverted ice-cream cone, much taller than it is broad. When people think about the governance structure of the Church of Scotland, what they are thinking can probably be expressed by those images.

For some, their experience is of national and regional agencies that support their local work and worship. Perhaps they have received a loan or grant from the Church's property-holding arm, the General Trustees, to help with a buildings difficulty. Perhaps they have had someone training for ministry serving a placement in their congregation, and gained an understanding of everything that goes into that process of formation. Perhaps they are using learning materials provided by the specialist writers who create them on-line for local use. Perhaps their Presbytery has run a youth event for their local town, something the local congregation is just too small to do by themselves. Their experience of the 'cone' is one of receiving resources and skills that cascade from what feels to them like a benevolent **centre**. For them, the imagined cone is the shallow one.

For others, their experience of the 'superior' courts of the Church feels like being oppressed from the **top**, not supported from a centre. Perhaps their congregation is facing the closure of a building they feel able to keep open, because of a policy that has led to the kind of difficult decision that is always easier to take when you are not emotionally invested. Perhaps the much-admired young adult they were sure should become a minister has not succeeded in assessment for reasons the congregation rightly do not know. Perhaps the level of contribution required from 121 next year to meet stipends and central administration costs has caused the blood to drain from every elder's face on hearing it. For them, the imagined cone is very tall and sharp.

No wonder, then, that serving part of a ministry in 121 really does still count as ministry. Like the civil service in a prosperous country, I suppose, it works to ensure the smooth running of a community that is locally focused on enterprise (mission) and community (discipleship). These are people who need the emotional intelligence to deal with distress that sometimes sounds like aggression, in situations in which they might have felt just the same way if the problem was in the congregation in which they worship. These are people who need to possess the creativity of thought, the flexibility of imagination, to find answers to tricky questions and so provide encouragement and confidence in places they may never have visited. Like any ministry, I suppose, this requires the thickness of skin to cope with people at their most unpleasantly defensive, and yet also the thinness of skin to be able to empathise with stress and anxiety in times of crisis. But this is also a ministry that allows a vicarious pleasure in the things that go well all over the Church, and a little satisfaction, perhaps, in being able to contribute to other people's triumphs.

One thing in particular deserves to be celebrated. It's often thought, quite wrongly, that ministers working in 121 are paid better than parish ministers. There are differences in view about manses, whether they are a benefit or a burden to occupy; that makes it difficult to compare jobs with such tied houses and those without. On most measures, though, very few ministers working at Assembly or Presbytery level are better off than they would be as parish ministers. Having moved from the parish to 121 and back again, my experience was that it was pretty income-neutral, and that was at a grading that was about average for the staff who are ordained ministers.

However, the point I want to make here is about the non-ministers who work in the central offices. Many of them provide expertise so specialist that they come from very highly-paid professions, include law, accountancy and architecture. Working for the Church, they receive *at best* the kind of remuneration of an in-house lawyer (or whatever) in public service. Most of them, I suspect, forfeit a great deal of income measured over decades of service which could have been given in the more lucrative private sector; and many of them do it as an act of Christian faith and commitment. I just want to put that out there.

You might think – especially if you have been trained to be suspicious of 121 as the pointy kind of cone – that it would be a dour, humourless machine of a place. In fact, some of the most bizarre 'you couldn't make this up' moments happen there or at the Assembly itself. Ask those who have come to work there without a church background whether it was what they expected.

A newish Head of Media Relations found herself fire-fighting the press interest in a disciplinary case that was being heard in public. We don't do that any more, thank goodness[14]. The case was somewhat, er, steamy, featuring lurid details and even at one point some physical evidence in the form of a piece of clothing. The local newspaper couldn't quite decide whether this was a 'hold the front page' moment, and reacted by sending a reporter all the way to Edinburgh *but* choosing their youngest staff member for the job. As the evidence unfolded (some of it literally), the Head of MR suddenly noticed out of the corner of her eye that the cub reporter had sprung a nose bleed with the shock of it all, and she had to take him away and tend to his wound.

The same colleague was appointed to that MR role just before the other General Assembly held away from our own Assembly Hall during the Parliament's tenancy. It seemed like a sensible idea to someone in Human Resources to appoint this lady's first day in the job to be the opening day of the General Assembly of 1999, held in the Edinburgh International Conference Centre. Whoever that was, they really hadn't thought it through.

I'm old-fashioned when it comes to buildings and ceremonial, believing that the dignity of the former serves the dignity of the latter. Whatever your view of the panoply of Church and State at the opening ceremony of the Assembly each May, the procession of the Lord High Commissioner and their suite up the flight of steps from New College Quad and on into the gallery behind the Moderator's chair certainly has an elegance and poise to it. It doesn't translate seamlessly into all other buildings, though.

---

[14] The change from the old brutal ways is mentioned in *Visions and Authorities,* Kindle Direct Publishing, 2023, pp 82-83 and 87-88

OH ALL RIGHT THEN

You might imagine the reaction of our newest colleague, therefore, as she stood on the upper level of the EICC not far from the top of one of the escalators, and suddenly saw a bunch of fully-robed ministers and lawyers (our Clerks' procession, which was a tradition back then) appearing inch by inch from our heads downwards as we ascended from our rooms below. That was nothing, though, to the Archers and Heralds, senior Scottish politicians and military figures preceding Their Graces, floating upwards into view, bows and arrows followed by tunics in the pattern of the Scottish Standard and batons (and forgive me that I've probably misnamed their esoteric equipment).

Apparently it is to my credit that, when I had ascended into her view, I winked at my new colleague to re-assure her; she did not turn and run, but decided to stay and embrace what might be the oddest and most fun-promising appointment she had ever had.

The Assembly, and its executive function in 121, does not spend all its time looking 'down' at the rest of the Church (or benevolently 'over' it if you are up for the flatter version of the cone metaphor). It also looks outwards to Scotland and the world. Whether it is the work of the Churches together enabling important conversations around the life of the Scottish Parliament, or statements from the Moderator at times of national joy or grief, or Reports brought to the Assembly on matters of deep international concern in the areas of justice and compassion, or the support of the huge army of school chaplains making connections with young people in their parishes, the Church provides a voice, a personality, a fund of resources at its centre to strengthen the message we all try to represent in our small corners.

This collection of stories and reflections on ministry has, until chapter 3, described quite a straight-line journey, from discernment of call through training and into the standard pattern of parish-based ministry. Sure, that in itself has the potential for challenging variety, for experiences that require the ability to think on your feet and extemporise your response, for routine that is sometimes delightful and sometimes dull, and for the non-routine that takes joy or anxiety to extremes.

However, this chapter has begun the job of introducing you to the world of other opportunities that exist alongside the things people probably think of when they think about a Church of Scotland minister. In our ordination vows, we promise to attend to those as part of the very core of what we do; the choice we have to make is to allow more of our time and energy to be taken by those things because our God-given abilities suit us to that work. In my experience, congregations are wonderfully accommodating of that. I think they recognise that it gives them a more fulfilled, satisfied and therefore content minister; and I suspect that they clock that it might provide them with some stories they would be the poorer not to hear.

'If you want something done, take it to someone who is busy,' is an aphorism that is irritating because it turns out to be true. 'You have a different stomach for pudding, and can manage one even if you didn't finish your main course,' is a mantra by which I often literally act. The ordination vow about playing your due part in the affairs of the General Assembly and Presbytery is not one that should be fulfilled grudgingly, minimally, resentfully. It is the offer of great gifts of experiences for you, and through you to your congregation and the wider Church you might be able to enrich.

About that Assembly in the EICC…

The Lord High Commissioner being the representative of the presence of the monarch, he or she was entitled to use a car without number plates for the duration of their Commission. The 'Palace party' would often attend the first part of a day's debates, and then depart to undertake a programme of VIP visits to Churches, projects, and so on.

OH ALL RIGHT THEN

Outside the EICC there is a small parking bay that should be used only for drop-offs. His Grace's chauffeur was waiting there for the party to appear from the hall at a suitable moment in proceedings, when two men approached from different directions. One was Very Rev Dr James Weatherhead, retired Principal Clerk, wit, and owner of a very serious face even when teasing. The other was a Council parking attendant (unkindly known locally as either 'blue meanies' or 'grey meanies', depending on the age of the story and consequently the colour of their jumpers).

Edinburgh's Finest announced to the chauffeur that if he didn't move that car he would receive a parking ticket. The former Principal Clerk quietly muttered that he really didn't want to do that. The Attendant decided he would have to make good on his threat, which of course required him to take the vehicle's registration number, didn't it? He inspected both ends of the car, in vain. Now he had to threaten much more serious legal proceedings. The former Principal Clerk quietly muttered that he really, *really* didn't want to do that, and should phone someone very senior in his chain of command and describe exactly where he was and what he was looking at. Happily for the chap's career, he did. All was well at last.

James being James though, a few moments later – when it was in fact clear that His Grace's suite was about to start moving – the debate of the morning was interrupted by a certain highly-respected former Moderator who said to the Assembly, 'If there is anyone present with a car without number plates, they probably need to go to it now, as there is a parking attendant standing beside it.'

Publicity photo as Acting Principal Clerk 2002

SERMON PREACHED WHILE WAITING FOR THE CHURCH TO DEBATE ANOTHER REPORT ON SEXUALITY

I have decided to reproduce this sermon, preached in May 2013, without bringing it up to date. I want to convey how a moment of history felt as we were living it and not knowing how it would resolve. This means that you must not read in it anything about the Church's current position, or that of civil law. For a more up-to-date account (in which you'll find some echoes of parts of this text) see Chapter 5 of 'Visions and Authorities'.

Tomorrow the General Assembly will debate the Report of its Theological Commission, will attempt to come to a conclusion on the theological question of whether individuals in civil partnerships may be ordained and inducted into the professional ministries of the Church, and will wrestle with the legal questions of how as a denomination we should move forward on this issue. Tension is high, nerves are jangling, people are excited or scared or both, careers and vocations are riding on what happens in Edinburgh.

I truly hope this will still seem something like a sermon, and not too much like a lecture squashed badly into an act of worship. But I think it might be helpful for those of you who know something extremely controversial and possibly damaging is happening in the Church you care about, and you want to understand it better.

Throughout my adult life the Church has debated the sexuality issue, sometimes loudly, sometimes quietly, sometimes inaudibly. Never has the Assembly made a pronouncement one way or the other. People on one side of the argument earnestly believe this silence means that the current position of the Church must be against allowing those in gay relationships to be leaders in the Church, because they are sure that was always the historical position and nothing has happened that has changed it. But people on the other side of the argument earnestly believe the silence means the Church neither approves nor condemns, because whenever it has failed to approve, it has also failed explicitly to condemn, so they would say you cannot describe the Church has having a formal rule one way or the other.

In 1993 the General Assembly were invited to instruct the disciplining of a minister who had conducted a service recognising the relationship of two women in her congregation. The Assembly declined to condemn the minister's action.

In 2006 when Civil Partnerships were new, the General Assembly were invited to authorise ministers to conduct services of blessing of such partnerships. The Assembly approved, but the measure had to be approved also by Presbyteries, because of its innovative and doctrinal nature, and it didn't receive enough support around the country. The following year's Assembly agreed that no decision could be said to have been made either for or against.

In 2009 the General Assembly were invited to forbid the induction to Queen's Cross Church in Aberdeen of the then minister of Brechin Cathedral. Believing that in a situation of such doubt they couldn't see that the Presbytery of Aberdeen was breaching any existing rule, the Assembly allowed the induction, but placed a moratorium on any further appointments and set up a Special Commission to bring a Report to the Assembly of 2011 recommending some kind of solution to the whole confusing debate.

In 2011 the Special Commission reported to the General Assembly, confessing that the expertise in their membership did not extend to the kind of theological knowledge that could have produced a report looking at the underlying theory of the question. They offered to the General Assembly the outline of two 'trajectories', as they called them, one a liberalising one that was called the 'Revisionist' trajectory, and the other a conservative one called the 'Traditionalist' trajectory, flawed titles but certainly the ones that are now common currency and you will hear them in the coverage of the coming days.

So the General Assembly in 2011 very provisionally opted for the Revisionist trajectory and set up a Theological Commission of seven theologians, most of them ministers including me. Our task was to examine the Revisionist trajectory under a theological light, and if possible bring proposals to this year's Assembly, but do so in a way that included safeguards for those in the Church who would be very uncomfortable with such a development.

In fact, because our Commission included such diversity of views, we too will bring Revisionist and Traditionalist proposals, this time with the theological arguments for each attached, and with legal proposals for how to take either of them forward if the Assembly choose to do so.

The dispute, unmissable within the Commission's meetings and endemic throughout the Church, would seem to be differences in the attitude we have to the authority of the Bible, for that is where people think they find the answer to this big current question. The Biblical arguments have been trotted out time and time again, so I'll spare you those and assume you know them. But when Paul tells Timothy that the Scriptures are breathed by God and useful for instruction, what do we take that to mean?

One school of thought in the Church is that the Bible has a plain meaning, a single meaning, and what it says can and should be directly applied and lived. Ask a proper Bible scholar about that, and they'll bury you under a heavy load of issues that make that a problem: cultural differences, our changing understanding of what life was like millennia ago, the complicated story of how the Biblical text was cobbled together from different competing sources, the lenses of our own culture and history and understanding and faith that so colour what we think we see. But that 'plain meaning of Scripture' faction tends to coincide quite extensively with those whom we call traditionalist on this question of human sexuality.

The opposite school of thought looks at the Bible as a jolly interesting collection of ancient documents that might even tell us something about the origins of our faith, *but that has no direct authority* to command what we do and think and believe. But listen to the witnesses to faith throughout 2000 years and they will talk to you of the vital accountability that comes from trying to be obedient to Scripture's words that are not just ordinary words, but that call us irresistibly, and lift us out of the temptation to choose only what we fancy in our Christian walk. So the attitude that does not acknowledge the 'authority' element will not do either.

On a bad day, and 20 May 2013 may be a bad day, everyone in the Church accuses those they disagree with of being at one or other of those extremes, and it's unfair to lots and lots of people to assume any such thing. For there are other, more nuanced, more intelligent, more sophisticated ways to read the Bible. I enjoyed recently a book by a Biblical teacher called Karl Allen Kuhn, who thinks of the Bible as the record of a conversation between God and the flawed, fragile, floundering People of God. The covers of your precious Bible can enclose the nightmare of a people believing their God would want them to murder the children of their enemies because they are human partners in the conversation despite getting things so very humanly wrong; and yet those same covers enclose the heavenly visions of the promises of Jesus Christ who gets nothing wrong. It is all important and it all shapes us and shapes our faith – but not 'simply'.

How does the Church find in the same way a nuanced, intelligent, balanced solution to this ghastly debate facing it right now?

The Commission's Report brings two alternative proposals, and each of them tries to be generous and not fundamentalist. The Revisionist proposal declares the eligibility of those in Civil Partnerships to enter the ministry.

OH ALL RIGHT THEN

But then it sets up lots of protections to ministers or Kirk Sessions to safeguard themselves against effects they would not be happy with. A Kirk Session therefore might agree in advance that the congregation's Nominating Committee would not consider applicants in that category; or a minister could be excused attending an induction in a neighbouring charge that would cause him or her difficulty. This tries to combine freedom with profound respect for differing views. It is, I suppose, premised on the principle that people should be allowed to be as strict as they like in applying their moral beliefs to themselves and their own immediate circles, but no-one has the right to try to over-ride the genuinely-held and long-prayed-through convictions of someone else – in either direction of this disagreement.

The Traditionalist proposal we are bringing allows for no further ordinations in that category, but very fairly accepts that those gay ministers who have been working in the Church since before the 2009 decision should not be disadvantaged by having a new rule applied retrospectively to drive them out of their careers. They would be free to continue to work, to develop their careers and to live their personal lives according to their consciences. And with the passing of time, gradually, their number will reduce through retirement, but with dignity.

As you follow the debate whose background I have sketched, I think I'm suggesting that you look at it as having several layers. The top layer is the presenting issue, the question about one category of ministers and deacons. The next layer down is that debate about the Bible, for we could be having a very similar argument about a completely different presenting issue, on, say, relations with other faith groups or something equally contentious, and in truth it would really have the same questions about the authority of Scripture lurking underneath the surface. I fear though that there is a third layer, rather a dark one, and deepest of all. Those who have a fundamentalist attitude to Scripture tend to end up judging others, their purity, their Christianity, even their salvation, because they think that is plain to read too in the lives they examine. Their rather binary attitude to truth allows them to see other people as 'in or out', always of course seeing themselves as 'in'.

They are like those Gileadites at the ford in the Jordan, trying to stop the escaping Ephraimites who were pretending to be anything but Ephraimites. Just as in the Second World War Americans in the Pacific War shot anyone who couldn't pronounce the letter 'L' assuming they were 'Japs', the Ephraimites didn't know how to pronounce the sound 'sh'; so when they were challenged by their Gileadite enemies to say the word that means 'ear of corn', 'shibboleth', they said 'sibboleth' and were summarily slaughtered in their tens of thousands.

The gay debate is today's shibboleth, standing for a cause that is about the place of the Word of God in the life of the Church, but in reality wielded by extremists on both sides of this debate – I'll say it again, on both sides of this debate – who want some people, their lives or their opinions, to be excluded from the community of Christ's people.

But, and here I am really trying to end in sermon and not lecture mode, Jesus Christ, in the middle of his most comforting piece of teaching, spoke of his Father's house having many rooms. How much has the Church come to terms with it not being one enormous room? How much has the Church learned to accept that perhaps Heaven has space enough, mansions enough, for a range of people too wide for us to manage here on earth?

And please God, may our Assembly remember that such a diversity includes those whose natures and lifestyles make this a scary time for them, but also those whose lifelong beliefs and conscience make them fearful too.

God bless them all, and all of us. Amen

5 STUDYING THINKING SPEAKING WRITING

'In that case', said Professor Forrester, 'come and do your PhD here.'

'But this isn't a Law Faculty', I stupidly remonstrated.

'No-one will notice', he replied.

By early 1999, layers of sediment had begun to build up in my ministry. I had a law degree that I had stopped using in the secular legal profession in my mid-20s; I had a few years of experience as a parish minister; I had just become Depute Clerk of the General Assembly full-time after a couple of years of juggling it part-time from Stromness; and I was once again living in Edinburgh with its University library in easy reach.

Doing a job that didn't scatter itself inefficiently across the diary in the way parish ministry does, I reckoned this was the moment to scratch one of my itches and do a part-time PhD. It would be nice, I thought, to do something that might exercise a little more of what I had studied in my law degree at Old College, Edinburgh, and combine it with my more recent divinity studies half a mile from there in New College.

OH ALL RIGHT THEN

Having served as Depute Clerk for a couple of years by that point, I could see that a cliff-edge was approaching in the legal relationship between Scotland's national Church and the British constitution. While grander figures and bigger brains than mine would decide the way ahead in an increasingly secular political and legal Establishment, it seemed worth researching something that would offer some historical context and a bit of material for future debate.

That, it seemed to me, made it a legal issue (or at least an issue in legal philosophy) more than a question of dogma or apologetics; and so I assumed the place I needed to pursue this was *Old* College. Now I possibly just picked the wrong person to ask, but the conversation I had there kept veering into Roman Catholic theories of Natural Law and Canon Law, and I felt I was getting nowhere fast. No-one understood!

Round to *New* College I went trailing my gloomy cloud behind me like a latter-day Linus. As soon as I came into the building, I had that familiar sense its graduates have of a place of welcome and belonging, a place where the people 'get' you and understand what your life of ministry is like. I found Duncan Forrester, then still active in the areas of Christian Ethics and Practical Theology, and told him my woes.

'In that case...', which is where we came in. And so I did.

There are at least three ways in which a Church of Scotland minister continues to be an intellectual figure long after they have completed their formation for ordination in a place like New College.

First of all, as in any profession, ministers need to keep current with academic developments in their field. Just as doctors read medical journals, lawyers read case reports, and teachers keep up to date with best practice, so ministers need to be engaged with the movements in theological and biblical studies that can change generational thinking. To the lay member that might seem a little odd, in a religion that claims stability and truth over a two thousand year history. But in my lifetime, for example, the Qumran Scrolls have transformed our understanding of the religious context of Jesus' era, Liberation Theology has swept part of the globe and then subsided again, Process Theology has changed the language used about Providence, and theories about the order in which New Testament books were written have changed and changed again. That list barely exemplifies world-wide theological scholarship and its lavish outpouring year by year. We owe it to those we teach in our pews to be ourselves engaged with the thinking of those clever academics whose job is to lead that thinking and track changes in understanding.

For instance, over the course of my ministry I have changed the way I refer to God in worship, using pronouns as little as possible these days. In a world where people's self-identity may be quite conflicted when it comes to gender (or indeed, might be terribly clear in ways that make other people feel conflicted!), it is impossible not to notice that Hebrew texts use masculine, feminine, neuter and even plural terms for God. Maybe it is not entirely 'biblical' to stick always with the masculine singular; perhaps using the language of fatherhood every week does not ease every spirit's journey towards faith? So if there is a way of referring to God without using 'He/Him/His', and it doesn't mangle the elegance of my prose or threaten the integrity of my own theology, that is how I will shape the thought. Equally, though, if the moment is one which I hope will resonate with the long tradition in which people here have their being (before a sermon, 'In the name of God: Father, Son and Holy Spirit') then I will honour that language and hope it is more uplifting than damaging to its hearers. But at least I think about it each time and try to get it right, and for me 'right' has changed a bit.

OH ALL RIGHT THEN

Three hundred years ago in our tradition, there was a strange argument about one of our confessional documents. The dispute concerned the question of whether God might shed new light on it for an improved understanding, or whether such an important text had to be understood only one way without the slightest change of approach even in changing circumstances. Of course, that kind of disagreement also lies behind debates about our interpretation of Scripture, and the nature of its authority over us, all around the Church. The point I am making here is just that we owe it to those we serve to be at least aware of what the 'new licht' looks like, and develop our own beliefs as seems to us to be right and obedient.

The second kind of mental endeavour of a parish minister is the historic task of being a local 'public intellectual'. Long ago, even in educationally-world-leading Scotland, literacy was limited and higher education was very rare. In parish-centred local communities, any writing of history, geography, geology, folk-lore, ideas of any kind, was in the hands of the minister and the schoolmaster/dominie and very few others. Look at the *Old*[15] and *New*[16] *Statistical Accounts* that cover every parish in Scotland (amongst the most useful reading you can do on arrival at a country parish, by the way), and you will find most of the entries are written by clergy. These men wrote with authority about the minutiae of agricultural practice and land quality, about rents, businesses and incomes, and about that area's place in history. These are encyclopaedic entries, far better than anything you would find in Wiki; and hundreds of ordained ministers of various denominations were trusted, *expected*, to be capable of that kind of writing.

Then, I suppose, more widespread education changed patterns of expertise and respect. The age of the polymath passed as more technical ages arrived, and more people

---

[15] Of the 1790s, available online these days.
[16] Of the 1830s and 1840s, and indeed initiated by a Scottish religious charity.

handled much more knowledge or ideas than could be retained in just one person's mind, and the minister and the dominie stopped seeming uniquely qualified to be the brains of the community.

I wonder, though, if things are changing again. As people spend as much time on untrustworthy social media feeds as their grandparents would have spent reading books, as dog-whistle populism teaches so many people to sneer at serious open-minded debate, as journalism is so often so partisan and nasty, as a cost of living crisis focuses the concern of so many people on their own most basic needs without capacity for a wider view of the world, I wonder whether there is once again a deficit of what you might call a virtuous, intelligent, *public* curiosity. The parish minister, who lives in (or these days, at least, near) the locality, may have a role to play as a 'verified' source of information, wisdom, stimulating ideas.

The third element of any minister's scholarship is in service of the Church as an institution, and I suppose some ministers are more heavily relied on for that than others. Churches constantly have to make complicated decisions about their own internal organisation, the method of their discipline, their corporate responses to the events of the world, their planning of activity, the gradual evolution of their standards of belief, and all sorts of other vital elements of corporate life and mission.

Look at the Reports from the General Assembly's committees each Spring, and you will be humbled by the expertise offered by our specialists in so many areas. Offering words for me to 'own', one colleague explains things about the Church in other countries of which I knew nothing, another minutely dissects a contentious public issue with a skill-set far beyond me, and of course others report on the expert handling of financial assets I would not want to touch with a ten-foot pole for fear of the mess I'd make of them. Maybe somewhere in there are a few words

OH ALL RIGHT THEN

I wrote about something in a small area of specialisation entrusted to me, and I give that little in return for receiving so much. The Church finds and applies knowledge and expertise where she finds them, so that as an institution of this world she may survive and thrive.

Look, too, at more sustained pieces of writing offered to generate debate that is needed and healthy. Browse the recent writings of Doug Gay in Glasgow University, Liam Fraser who chairs our Theological Forum, and Neil Glover in Aberfeldy; all of them write passionately about the life of our Church from positions of deep scholarship and thorough knowledge of our past and present ways. Like me in a piece like this one, they offer ideas that may dismay or shock some people; that is a mark of success if it means important discussion in the smallest corners of parish life or Presbytery committees.

None of those three intellectual roles requires anyone to undertake postgraduate work, and it is probably becoming more and more difficult to fit that kind of time commitment for study in to ministries that are expanding through the current processes of resource-restructuring. That is a pity.

For those who can still find a way to study further, the opportunities span both kinds of postgraduate study: research degrees and taught degrees. The range of available Masters Degrees is vast, especially now that online study has removed most geographical constraints; and many of these combine an element of teaching input with the chance to write a dissertation on something that has useful application in your own ministry.

At doctoral level, there are two main ways to proceed. One is the conventional Doctor of Philosophy (PhD) route I took, in which the substantive output is a book-length thesis that makes an original contribution to scholarship on your topic. You could say that the award of a PhD is the Academy's way of declaring you are now an official expert in something; the something might be very small, and it may be something no-one else cares a fig about, but that almost doesn't matter.

The other way forward is a 'professional' doctorate, often in the form of the Doctor of Ministry (DMin) degree now offered by some Scottish Universities in collaboration with various American providers who have longer experience in this kind of course. These degrees involve a cohort of ministers (and others) studying together through seminars, presentations and short papers, and culminate in one longer dissertation on a ministry-related topic.

Long ago, when the Church mattered in the academic world, the ancient Scottish universities awarded honorary Doctor of Divinity degrees (DD) to quite a few ministers. Today they are very rare indeed, almost unheard-of beyond the ranks of former Moderators. Way back then, the DD was often in recognition of the 'public intellectual' role I've described, and would follow the publication of a well-researched volume of local history, or an intelligent contribution to a hot topic of religious debate. I like to think that the DMin degrees earned by some of the most energetic of my colleagues are our generation's equivalent of the DD; they mark out those ministers who recognise their calling as partly an academic one even in the thick of the busy-ness and practicality of ministry.

Back to my PhD, and another of my couldn't-make-this-up moments. As part of my original research I was conducting what are known as 'elite interviews'. Instead of surveying lots and lots of people to get statistical reliability from the big sample, you are interviewing just a few people who are very prominent in a field because it is the quality of their wisdom and not a weight of many opinions that you want. Well, my topic was the interface of the civil and spiritual legal jurisdictions of Church and State (yawn), and my interviewees included the Principal Clerk, the Procurator of the General Assembly, some constitutional law experts… and for good measure Lord Mackay of Clashfern, the former Lord Chancellor and one of the most friendly and prominent Christians in political life. Off I nervously went to the Houses of Parliament with my recording equipment – and it was the size that sort of gear was in the early 2000s.

I had received a message from Lord Mackay, explaining that his own office in the House of Lords was being refurbished, but that one of his colleagues was going to lend us his office which would provide the peace and quiet I would need to make the recording. It was the size of a walk-in cupboard, containing one table, one chair, one bookcase, and a window that looked straight across to the Elizabeth Tower containing some famous bells. His Lordship, a gentleman as well as a Christian, insisted that I occupy the table and chair because of the microphone and so on; and, setting carefully to one side his friend's books and papers on the window-sill, the former Lord Chancellor of Great Britain clambered onto it and invited me to begin, the famous clock face peeping over his shoulder. Every fifteen minutes throughout our conversation, Big Ben bonged his way into my recording, and – resisting the urge to pinch myself – I thought that New College, once again, had utterly failed in its preparation of me for the moment.

The ways of 'giving back' the treasures of life-long learning are manifold in our ministry. Gone, perhaps, are the days of the parish minister writing the local entry for the Statistical Account. It is still, though, the weekly bread-and-butter job of the regular preacher to enrich the congregation's encounter with Scripture, filling out a reading with its context, its historical setting, its political and religious background, the vast metadata of its original language or its references to other passages, or its use and abuse by the Church throughout Christian history. And that teaching role might extend to parish study groups, Alpha (and its various competitors) and the didactic elements of school chaplaincy.

OH ALL RIGHT THEN

Many ministers find themselves asked to contribute something more specific, depending on the specialist knowledge and experience they might happen to have; it always feels like a bit of a burden to be asked… but eventually you are awfully glad you were given the opportunity and the fun encounters that probably came with it. I can think of three ways I have exercised the grey matter at other people's invitation.

After I finished that PhD, graduating in 2004, I wondered (typically of people at that stage) whether I could publish any of what I had written. Part of the problem was that my thesis had analysed a court case that had not quite finished by the time I had submitted my work for the degree. It was rather frustrating.

Enter the Trustees of the Chalmers Lectureship. Churches are amongst the institutions of society that have many trusts and charities connected to them, and amongst those trusts are endowed lectureships. An endowed lectureship need not belong to a university; it is a trust fund that appoints someone from time to time to deliver some public lectures on a theme that the trust exists to promote (it might be foreign mission, or ecumenical relations, or whatever). And often the terms of the trust facilitate the publishing of the lectures as an academic volume after they have been delivered.

The Chalmers Lectureship, named after the Disruption leader Thomas Chalmers, exists to explore the concept of the 'headship of Christ over His Church', which meant it was not difficult to shoehorn my PhD–on church law, authority and governance–into the purposes of the trust. I was appointed Lecturer for its standard four year term from 2004-2008, on the understanding that I would deliver the lectures as late as possible in the cycle. By 2007 the knotty case had finally ended, and I was able to reach some proper conclusions about its implications for the Church's legal position. I stripped back my 100,000 word thesis to six

lectures each of about 6,000 words (I'm afraid the elite
interviews did not make any explicit experience, not even
Big Ben's bongs), delivered the lectures in the theological
schools at Glasgow and Aberdeen[17], and then wrote the
monograph published in 2009 under the same title as the
thesis, *The Crown Rights of the Redeemer*[18]. The final book was
a mixture of the still-useable chapters of the thesis and the
much-updated description of more recent events from the
lectures.

A second example of the pull of the academic came
much more recently. New College[19] had the inspired idea
of appointing six of its more ancient ordained graduates as
'Fellows', an ecclesiastical appointment rather than a
university one (see footnote to explain that distinction). We

---

[17] Hats off to the Master of Christ's College Aberdeen who unilaterally
instructed the Church candidates there that attendance at my lectures was one
of his requirements of their ministerial formation. What a difference it made to
the size of the audience.

[18] The title, I confess, was a bit naughty. 'The Crown Rights of the Redeemer'
was one of the slogans of the Covenanting movement in the seventeenth
century. Anything less like a radical anti-establishment Covenanter than me is
hard to imagine. So I admit I picked a title that would tease those who would
not expect me to pin my colours to such a mast. At the time of writing there
is precisely one second-hand copy of *Crown Rights* available on Amazon.
Airport book-stand blockbuster it was not; but that was not its purpose. I
wouldn't bother looking for it if I were you.

[19] There are five university theology ('divinity' is the more common term in
Scotland) schools amongst the Church's training providers. One, St Andrews,
always had a single institution with no academic split at the time of the
Disruption, so it is known as 'St Mary's College' both within the University and
for the Church's purposes. One, in the University of the Highlands and Islands,
is far too modern to have tangled with Scottish Church History at all. The other
three, in Aberdeen, Glasgow and Edinburgh (listing them in age order), each
went through a period of competing Church of Scotland and Free Church
colleges; each eventually united the two in the 1920s but was left with
discernibly separate academic and ecclesiastical structures and leadership. So
in Aberdeen the divinity faculty is known for Church purposes as Christ's
College, whose 'Master' is a Church appointee concerned with all-round
formation of the Church's ordinands for ministry. In the same way Edinburgh's
'New College' and Glasgow's 'Trinity College' each have a Principal who is the
equivalent of Aberdeen's Master.

are ministers trained there long ago, with lots of parish experience and fairly hefty CVs in other ways too. In the nicest possible way, we are the Swiss army knives of the Principal and her colleagues: we engage with candidates, provide sounding-boards to them, give bits of academic input in the areas the Church likes to call 'praxis' which just means creative wobbling between theory and practice, and help the College to reach out from its normal student base to help practitioners across the Church in their own continuing academic discipline.

I seem to have cornered the market in one of the seminars in our students' course on 'Church, Sacraments and Ministry', a session on the tensions of the identity of a minister as both a set-apart ordained functionary and a living, breathing human being.[20] My colleagues doubtless have their own niches in other areas of the curriculum.

Recently I helped to supervise an Honours candidate writing a dissertation on a topic I was able to discuss with her; I don't think I did more than check she hadn't missed out on some important reading, but *mony a little maks a muckle*, so maybe I was of some benefit.

And from that appointment sprang the third kind of challenge. As part of its outreach programme, helping ministers and others to keep their professional practice reflective, New College offers short evening courses for the Church community. In 2023, I was given the opportunity to deliver something about the Church's 'mission', and the four-session evening class that emerged in the autumn turned into the book *Visions and Authorities*[21] already mentioned. The inverted commas round the word 'mission' in the previous sentence is a clue to that volume's starting-point, the slipperiness of a word that is either vague or

---

[20] In chapter 8 you'll get the guts of what I say to them on this.
[21] KDP, 2023, which you'll find alongside this volume on Amazon. If you have been mesmerised, or even just traumatised, by the Church's recent mission planning process (sic), that book might be worth a skim.

weaponised in much of its use; the book really asks how the Church goes about finding a *non*-vague, *non*-weaponised, better definition of what she should be doing. I don't offer the answer; it was all I could do to wrangle the *process* into words.

It was when I thought about the publishing of *Visions* that I made the discovery of Amazon Kindle's tool for independent publishing; if you have an Amazon account you are just a few clicks (in the depths of the long menu) from becoming a 'Kindle Direct' author. With no upfront costs, and no delays because no third-party publisher, we have entered a new era by which someone with something to say in written form can place it in front of a readership of their choosing almost as soon as the thought has formed. And so the last example of sustained writing as an element of ministry is the book in your hands now, written in corners of non-working days with only my own memory as my research. It would be fun to see twenty ministers write their own versions of this piece, with stories as daft as mine but completely different. I dare them.

Royal Naval Reserve, No 1 Rig

SERMON (READINGS: THE SACRIFICE OF ISAAC, AND THE PARABLE OF THE SHEEP AND GOATS)

Picture the scene; three Church of Scotland ministers on holiday in a chalet at Crieff Hydro many years ago, and we are playing Trivial Pursuit. Trivial Pursuit, as you know, is an irritating game because the answer-cards are not always correct – for instance the original edition claimed that the Tay is the longest river in England – and the players end up having arguments about whether the correct answer is the one on the card, or the real answer that everyone knows it is. On this occasion the minister of Newtyle has made a wild guess at one of those questions so obscure no-one has a hope with it (about sport, or science, or something) and I, holding the card, have read out the answer exactly as it is given on the back. We are feeling no more illuminated by the answer than we were by the question. The minister of Newtyle, who is feeling just a little piqued, challenges me, 'How can that possibly be the answer to that question? What do you mean? Explain what you mean!' And I hear myself say, 'Don't ask me for explanations; I've only got the answers.' And there is a little pause, and my two companions say, in perfect chorus, 'Preach on that, preach on **Don't ask me for explanations, I've only got the answers**.'

And I did, all those years ago, and it's a tension that presents itself afresh every time I come face to face in the lectionary with a text I wish I didn't have to tackle in the pulpit, like Abraham offering to sacrifice Isaac.

I very firmly believe that there are parts of the Christian story that just don't support explanation. If you believe that everything written in the Bible literally happened, you must have to tie yourself in knots to work out how the God and Father of Jesus Christ would have directed that scene of

105

OH ALL RIGHT THEN

Abraham preparing to stick a knife in the only son he had longed for all his long life. Surely our task with the story is not to explain it as it stands, but to contemplate what it would mean to have an obedience to God beyond everything else we hold dear, to have a trust in God that wouldn't give up when things seemed to make least sense, to have a faith in God that was willing to go into the most unfamiliar and frightening experiences.

So I suppose I take the easy way out of all this muddle and puzzle. I have long since convinced myself that there are questions which the human race does not have it in us to answer. There are aspects of the truth about God which are more complicated than our brains have capacity to grasp. There are dimensions to Christ and the glory of Christ which are beyond the four dimensions of space and time in which we measure things in our earthly experience. In other words, aren't there things which we are simply not intended to understand? They are thrown in our path precisely so that we will puzzle over them and get nowhere and have to resort to faith and hope and imagination and poetry and stories and needing God. These are the mysteries that so tantalise us that faith is the only way of coping with them. These are the big questions that make us look for the answers even though we are hard put to it to dream up explanations.

There are the people who like to have the answers to religious questions and who do not care tuppence about having explanations; and there are other people, who can't help ferreting about for explanations and can't bear anything that seems to them an over-easy answer. The Church must own up to both of these kinds of people and let them be what they are, whatever they are.

So within the Body of Christ there are many men and women who have a great single-mindedness of trust and certainty, who seize the faith wholeheartedly and have no desire to take it to pieces and examine it bit by bit. There is

106

no element of scientific method to their believing, and indeed why should there be? They are enormously lucky in one way because the whole package of Christian doctrine makes equal sense to them – it's all one piece as far as they are concerned.

Those 'answers' people can suffer two kinds of pain. It hurts them, first, when they come across people who are not like them, when they see other churchmen and women tinkering with the faith, doubting bits of it, throwing out bits of it, redefining bits of it. But they don't need that kind of messing about with religion, as they would see it, and so they say, 'Don't ask me for explanations; I've got the answers.' They become upset because it seems to them that asking for explanations seems insolent or even a little blasphemous. *There* is the faith; why can't other people just take it on trust as they do?

The second kind of pain they suffer is the burden their monolithic doctrines gives them. When something happens that shakes them, so that one part of their religious conviction gets a bit damaged, sometimes the whole edifice goes at once. It is often those very certain, confident Christians who turn up just a short time later having completely abandoned the faith. They can't cope with the discovery that their Gospel is not impregnable, that their faith hasn't dealt with everything thrown at it. It's all or nothing.

In the other part of the Body of Christ are the people who want the explanations before they will accept the answers. Some people's minds work that way; they have to know how and why before they will consider the 'whether'. So they need to know where some piece of doctrine has come from before they will bring judgement on it and decide whether to commit themselves such an article of faith. Doctrine is accepted on merit, not just because it's said with authority. They demand the explanations, and they feel troubled on days like today when the stories are difficult or hard to hear, and the Church fails to satisfy their curiosity.

These 'explanations' folk have a choice to make. They can give up in frustration, and give the Church up as a bad job. The Bible has just too many hard words in it, or the Christians they see live lives that don't convince them there is a beautiful truth in there somewhere, or God has too many dimensions and too many of them are dark and forbidding. It all makes too little sense, and doesn't seem worth the bother.

Or they can throw open their arms and revel in a world of faith where the depths of meaning are bottomless, where a sense of mystery carries us through the parts of life that defy easy pigeon-holing, where the sheer breadth of Christian experience lets us survive the worst that happens to us because we see it together with the best and noblest of our experiences. People who need explanations before they will feel fully committed to the Gospel of Jesus Christ probably need to realise that they will never get to the end of the hunt for explanations, and so they will never stop reviewing their commitment and their place in the drama of God's unfolding history.

Thank goodness, then, for passages like today's Gospel, the words from Matthew that seem so much more immediate. When people welcome us as Jesus' followers, they welcome him, and when they welcome him they welcome God. We can 'get' that; we don't wriggle and squirm and feel hot under the collar when we hear those words. But then, stopping for a little moment to think about them, is it not every bit as much of a challenge and a mystery to act out that text as it is to get our heads round the hardest and most violent Old Testament stories? When it gets simpler, it certainly doesn't get easier, but neither does it become less worthwhile.

There is so much to puzzle over, so much to ask God to help us work out, so much that will spill from thought into longing and from longing into prayer. There are questions, and then there is the way we answer them. There are others sharing our world and the Church, who answer them differently. What we need to learn is the gentleness with which Christ approached human beings, however he encountered them. We need that gentleness to deal with dignity with those we cannot begin to understand, to endure with humour those who cannot begin to understand us.

Whether you have the questions and answers all buttoned up, and your 'faith believes nor questions how', or whether answers alone do not stimulate you unless you can explore and explode them, and ''twixt gleams of joy and clouds of doubts your feelings come and go', be aware that you share the puzzle of our great and glorious faith with many who are unlike you. Perhaps amongst us we can perceive the answers, and find some of the explanations.

6 ROYAL NAVAL RESERVE

In the autumn of 2010, the RAF transport plane
dropped like a stone from the central Asian sky and landed
on the dark runway of Kabul Airport.[22]   It felt like the
highest and lowest point of my career in the Royal Naval
Reserve, and I knew I wouldn't take off again from that strip
of tarmac and head home for another three months.
Waiting for me on the 'military' side of the airport was
Sheila, the chaplain I was to replace as Kabul Garrison
Chaplain[23], along with the Adjutant of Camp Souter and the
usual convoy of two ridgeback vehicles and six soldiers

---

[22] For reasons I trusted at the time, but were not shared by other nations
involved in the ISAF operation, British policy was to perform air-moves of
personnel in the middle of the night, and to use sickening descent-angles for
landings, in both cases to minimise the risk of anti-aircraft action by those who
did not want us there. It brought a whole new level to ear-popping.

[23] Interestingly, Rev Sheila Munro was at the time the only female Church of
Scotland Chaplain in the RAF, while I was the only one in the Royal Navy. I
suppose our Church had two very scarce eggs in one rather dodgy basket for
a few hours. She is probably the most affectionate chaplain I've ever seen at
work; the guys and girls must have felt they had brought their mum with them.

from 2 Signals who would bring us home to the camp by the three-quarters-of-a-mile, three-quarters-of-an-hour route to safety.

In the back of the ridgeback, a vehicle so well-armoured that its driver had to use CCTV to see where he was going, we were strapped in using four-point seatbelts to keep us in place if we were to happen to turn upside down, and wore goggles and gloves to prevent spall injury. Facing each other across the width of the cabin, our view of one another was interrupted by the legs of one of the soldiers, a Gurkha, whose top half was sticking out of the roof of the vehicle and tending our General Purpose Machine Gun. You could feel the few moments we halted while Souter gate guards checked underneath our chassis for anything unfriendly that might have, er, become attached during our journey.

So how did I get there, 'there' being a country with no coast line and 'I' being a *naval* chaplain of all things?

Chaplaincy in the Armed Forces is one of the most challenging, satisfying and broadening kinds of ministry, because it consists of caring for part of the demographic that is least represented in the civilian Church: young, healthy adults with a huge range of ability and life-experience.

I know about chaplaincy in the Royal Navy, and I'll trust readers to allow for the differences between it and the other two Services. We matelots have much less of a rank-structure, and when ashore wear uniform less often than the others do (in the tri-service and operational environment that was Op HERRICK in Afghanistan, that practice did not pertain, obviously – see the photo with Sunny on p125).

There are clear differences between military and civilian ministry too. The official definition of a Naval chaplain is 'friend and adviser to all on board, and an advocate for those of all faiths and none'; read very carefully, that means that the very core of our calling as ministers is technically an add-on to the much less confessional core of our role as chaplains, which takes a bit of juggling.

Some of the differences are very welcome. Someone else probably has to worry about the buildings in which you work, and you don't need to find a squad of volunteers either to take care of your family's home. There's a great deal more team-working in chaplaincy than we've quite managed to introduce in our parish ministry even in our 'new normal'. And while it's difficult to compare very differently-structured remuneration systems, it's probably true that I was better off in the year when I was mobilised in full-time service than I was in the parish ministry that followed.

The attentive reader will have spotted that in 1998 I left pastoral ministry for the full-time job in 121, and that involved losing a big part of what I'd felt called to be and do right back at the outset of my ministry journey. I felt uneasy not to be someone's minister, when I'd spent almost as long training for that role as I had spent so far doing it. (The military term for that is 'return of service', and I certainly felt then that I'd fallen rather short in making a return for all the training input I'd received.)

Meanwhile, somewhere quite deep down and never admitted out loud, there was another itch to scratch. Had I not been the kind of child – or perhaps I mean a child in the kind of family – for whom a university degree was the natural step after leaving school, I always thought I might have become a soldier or, more likely, a sailor.

When the Volume of Reports to the General Assembly was published in April 2004, the very month in which I had my PhD viva and wondered what to do next with my spare time, I read in the HM Forces Chaplaincy Report that the Royal Navy had decided to reconstitute the Chaplaincy Branch in the Maritime Reserves after a ten year gap. By November of that year, I had somehow negotiated all the preliminary steps of recruitment –including joining a gym –

and presented myself at the Admiralty Interview Board (think of a cross between (a) the National Assessment for CofS ministers and (b) one of the wetter challenges on *Gladiators*, and you're close enough). By March of 2005 I was being introduced to the unit that was to be my Thursday evening home for the next twelve years, HMS SCOTIA in Rosyth.

Now I confess I may not have researched all this *quite* as carefully as I should, and blundered my way through selection with rather an inaccurate idea of what the job was. I somehow imagined that I was volunteering to be chaplain *to* the RNR, rather as one might be chaplain *to* a cadet unit or a school. I visualised rocking up from time to time to do the religious bit and encourage the Ship's Company as they, ie other people, did the unpleasant stuff like PT, regular medicals, First Aid classes, fire-fighting training... and actually going to dangerous places.

But just to be clear, and how wrong I therefore was, a Reservist chaplain is ministering *within* their Service, as a full member and with all the training commitments, mobilisation liability and operational responsibilities as if you were a logistics officer or a submarine controller or the Ship's First Lieutenant. I had my 24-day-a-year commitment, 2.4 km run to complete annually, equality and diversity training, ceremonial commitments, the lot.

The initial training, which I completed over three years but which more recently has been compressed into a shorter time-frame, involved three fortnights of learning.

(There is a saying in the Reserves. *Ginger Rogers did everything that Fred Astaire did, but backwards and in high heels. A Reservist does everything that a Regular does, but does it all in a fortnight.* Few regulars would agree with us, as they do all sorts of things we don't. But when half of each year's commitment comes in the form of a two-week course, a great deal is packed in and you know you've been working hard by the end of it.)

The first fortnight was spent in a training base in Gosport, shadowing a chaplain from the same Church tradition, and learning everything from what to wear, what the gold stripes and anchors meant on what other people were wearing, and when (if at all) to salute, to approximately how the whole Navy is constructed.

The second fortnight was spent doing the RNR Junior Officers' course at the Britannia Royal Naval College in Dartmouth. I was old enough to be some of the other students' mother, shamelessly traded tasks ("you carry that pine pole from there to there, and I'll write the speech you're supposed to make"), and remember still the shredded state of my knees at the end of it all despite all the evasion techniques.

The third year's fortnight of training was the five day Basic Sea Safety Training course, and then a week and a half at sea in friendly domestic waters learning the (almost literal) ropes under the mentoring of what the Navy calls your 'Sea Daddy', the experienced member of the same branch who takes you under their wing and stops you doing anything completely stupid.

A story from November 2006, BRNC Dartmouth, and in particular the vast parade ground in front of the splendid frontage and terrace of the college.

One size fits all, which means that even a baby Bish[24] has to endure parade training, being spared only the sword-drill element of it since chaplains don't bear arms. Truth to tell, the whole thing is a bit of a waste of time. Any RN

---

[24] That takes a bit of getting used to, being called the Bish. Traditionally, RN ratings say Bish, naval officers say Chaplain, and the other Services say Padre. In recent years, with more Naval Officers being Upper Yardsman (those who come up from the ranks, what the Army would call 'career commissions') 'Bish' has crept into the mouths of officers. And with so many tri-service operations like HERRICK, naval chaplains have had to learn to be called 'Padre', which let me tell you takes even more getting used to for a cisgender female.

chaplain worth his or her salt will, when faced with any Divisions[25] that might involve marching, volunteer to say a prayer, give a blessing, or otherwise do something that requires them to dress in pulpit robes and stand on the dais with the inspecting officer. An entire career can pass without the chaplain ever having to march in a squad anywhere, which honestly is for the best for everyone.

With that hint in mind, you will imagine just how well I (the only chaplain in the group) was doing amongst my classmates in our drill training. Turning 'on the march' was a particular nightmare, in which I seemed bent on tripping one of my ankles with the other. Eventually we came to a shambling halt, waiting for the loud pearls of wisdom of the Royal Marine Sergeant who had drawn us as his short straw. But in the nick of time a running figure shot down from the terrace and whispered something to the Sergeant, who marched round behind the rear rank in which I thought I'd managed to hide myself from too much of his view. I stopped breathing and wondered if I was being dismissed from the course there and then. I wouldn't have blamed them.

But no.

'Fall yourself out, Ma'am. There's another God-botherer here to see you.'

I legged it gratefully to the terrace, where I was met by a kindly-looking stranger in a dog-collar.

'How do you do. I'm the Principal Roman Catholic Chaplain. I'm in the area on business, heard there was a chaplain-in-training here, and thought I'd come and see how you're getting on. I've been watching your parade drill, and thought you might prefer a cup of tea?'

I mentioned that Naval Chaplaincy doesn't have much of a rank-system. That means that we are unique in having no promotions to pursue early in our careers. That's

---

[25] Divisions is Jackspeak for many kinds of parade.

significant in the Reserves, where in every other branch they train every year to inch towards the next rank or rate. Once the initial matrix of training I've listed is complete, chaplains have no branch-specific training still to do, except to prepare for particular deployments as they crop up. That provides the RN with the gift of two weeks of highly-trained, ordained resource in quiet years, which can be used to provide some actual value somewhere.

So from the fourth year onwards, I had the most fascinating (and well-paid) summer adventures.

Usually it meant providing cover in a large shore establishment during the summer leave period, to allow the regular chaplains to have their own holidays. Places like HMS DRAKE (the shore base in Plymouth) or HMS RALEIGH (the Phase 1 training establishment for brand new ratings) do not completely close, so there are always some pastoral cases, weddings or baptisms to be handled. And always there is a duty chaplain, available 24 hours a day for emergencies in a setting where the chance of work-related accidents, off-duty mishaps or self-harm is higher than in most other concentrations of youngish adults.

In one of those 'locuming' stints, I wonder if I perhaps won the prize for being the least qualified person ever to work at the Royal Marines Commando Training Centre at Lympstone. I was 53 at the time, surrounded by men whose fitness and fighting skills were frankly terrifying. Even my fellow chaplains were rather daunting in that regard. One young Anglican priest would say to me, each morning, 'I'm going to have a swim instead of lunch today; would you like to come too?' And I would faithfully reply to him, each morning, 'The only problem I have with your sentence is the word 'instead'. I shall be buying sandwiches from the NAAFI and eating them outside in the sun; would you like me to get you anything while you're gone?' I mean, honestly, can you imagine what I'd have looked like in *that* company, in that pool? Come to think of it, don't.

OH ALL RIGHT THEN

The most significant liability of every Reservist, though, is the possibility of being mobilised for a period into full-time service. Your civilian employer (the Church, technically, doesn't 'employ' its parish ministers, but is treated as if it does for this purpose) must agree at the outset to this possibility, though at the point of call-up there is some consultation so that any impact (for instance in terms of timing) is not needlessly disruptive. The need for mobilisation in different Services and branches varies over time, depending on the needs of the regular Services; when Op TELIC (Iraq) and Op HERRICK (Afghanistan) were in full flow, many branches in every Service were at full stretch, and needed to call on Reservists to serve either in the front line of those deployments or in other more routine work to release Regulars to go where they were most needed.

I had found myself as the first Chaplain to join the RNR when the branch was 'stood back up' in 2004, and in 2010 I found myself as the first to be mobilised, in a natural gap in my career after my work for the General Assembly had ended and before I looked for a new parish ministry. Over a period of about eight months which officially began, by chance, on my 48th birthday, I did three things. The first, Op OCEAN SHIELD, is described in the next section, and you could call that a back-fill to cover another chaplain's normal role. The second was editing a collection of services to be used by ships at sea when there was no chaplain embarked; I did that from home for about a month between my deployments. The third was where this chapter started, Op HERRICK in Afghanistan.

HMS CHATHAM was one of the last Type 22 frigates used by the Royal Navy, and in the summer of 2010 was on her last deployment, Op OCEAN SHIELD, as the flagship of the NATO anti-piracy operations in the Indian Ocean. Co-ordinating an international task force of naval assets, we were trying to keep safe a route between the Bab-el-Mandeb

OH ALL RIGHT THEN

Strait and the west coast of India, known as the Internationally Recognised Transit Corridor (IRTC). We were also trying to support the policing operations on the coast of Somalia, where many of the pirate groups were based. For much of the time, our job was just to be seen to be there (you might say a lot like ministry in some ways I suppose); during the ship's deployment there were no pirate attacks within 100 nautical miles of her position in the IRTC. That meant though that by definition the action and danger were normally wherever we *weren't*, so the Ship's Company were working hard but not experiencing very much excitement. Sometimes the Chaplain's job is to remind people how worthwhile their work is at times when it is not very stimulating.

One of the greatest challenges I encountered – this time not so much 'New College didn't prepare me for this' as 'Dartmouth didn't prepare me for this' – was just getting into bed. Let me try to explain this.

I had embarked in Oman, a few weeks before the end of the ship's deployment. Because she was the flagship of the operation, she had some extra officers on board from different nations, and that meant she did not have a spare cabin for a newly-arrived Chaplain for my first ten days. There was a berth, in the six-person female Senior Ratings' cabin. The cabin was fourteen feet by seven by seven, contained two triple-decker bunks, and was home to three Petty Officers and one Chief Petty Officer who occupied the two lowest and two middle bunks, leaving me with a choice of either top bunk. I am 5'8". My bunk was at the height of my ear, and if you make a fist and measure the distance from your elbow to your knuckles, that was the space between my mattress and the deckhead[26]. To get in to the bed I couldn't climb up the lower bunks because that would disturb my shipmates; but cheerily there was a grab-handle screwed to the said deckhead allowing me to swing

---

[26] Jackspeak for ceiling. Deck is floor, bulkhead is wall.

that 48-year-old body up like an Olympic gymnast and then fire myself feet-first (like Suranne Jones going into the torpedo tube in *Vigil*) into that tiny space. Forget about sitting up in bed. Oh, and yes, I *do* have to get up in the middle of the night to go to the loo.

Afghanistan, on the other hand, was ministry in a war zone. Being at war, depending where exactly you find yourself of course, can consist of 95% boredom and 5% fear. And chaplaincy there consists I think of helping people to continue to be multi-dimensional human beings and not defined only by the difficult task they are there to fulfil.

Chaplaincy in Kabul was like this:

• visiting soldiers up in the sangars[27] at night, my side pockets stuffed with Mars Bars from the NAAFI shop for them. Sheila had told me it was a good way to have deeper conversations with the more junior personnel one by one, as they wouldn't open up in other places where their mates would hear them. I had to be in full body armour and helmet to do it, as I would be literally sticking my head above a parapet in each place, and I took a little torch to ensure the path from one tower to the next didn't contain any lurking camel spiders[28]

• from the dramatic to the ridiculous, being the personal shopper of all the female personnel, whose undies were routinely destroyed by a brutal laundry system. Many of them were in roles that meant they never left camp (you didn't, ever, if you didn't need to), but the only shop that sold smalls was the German Army's PX shop back at the airport which I visited once a week to see the British personnel serving up there. I would set off with a notebook full of codes like '3x34B', '2x38C' and a fistful of US dollars

---

[27] The watchtowers on the camp's perimeter wire
[28] I don't do spiders. But that's OK because these things weren't spiders. No, they were scorpions.

- from the ridiculous to the poignant, conducting the Remembrance Sunday parade for hundreds of personnel, attended by the Ambassadors from several Commonwealth countries. I read them a poem written by a POW who in the early 1940s was as young as many of them were now, and I didn't mention he was my father because they didn't need to know that. A brigadier at lunch asked where I'd found such an interesting old soldier

- from the poignant to the utterly delightful, as I found enough courage to give one of the dog handlers my camera and tentatively took from her the lead of 'Sunny the not very bitey bitey-dog', who (I was assured) had done the training that told him that anyone wearing Multi-Terrain-Pattern uniform was 'friend' not 'foe' so really I'd be OK.[29] The photo I'll share with you of Sunny and me is my favourite photo of myself ever.

Long after I returned from mobilised service to the relative peace of the Reserves, and five years into my ministry in the Carse of Gowrie, I had one final opportunity for a bit of sea time by giving a month rather than a fortnight in the summer of 2016. HMS ENTERPRISE was a hydrographic survey vessel which had been repurposed to serve in Op LITTEN, an EU operation this time, doing migrant rescue work in the part of the western Mediterranean between the Bay of Tripoli and the Italian coast. There were quiet days of waiting for something to happen, interspersed with a few busy days when everything happened.

It would begin at first light, because the smugglers would push the inflatables off the Libyan beaches under cover of darkness, giving the migrants the cooler hours of the night to reach international waters before running out of fuel and

---

[29] My faith in that training system did require a bit of courage. Only six weeks earlier we had switched from the old desert-pattern kit to the new MTP; had Sunny definitely got the memo?

waiting in hope of being spotted by the planes of the Italian Navy. If ENTERPRISE was the nearest asset to one of the boats, our Italian colleagues would direct us to the spot, and there would be the telling pipe throughout the ship 'Hands to SOLAS stations'.[30]

At that point the distribution of tasks was quite curious. Some specialities did their accustomed thing: so chefs cooked; and Marines stood to their machine-guns to ensure none of the little boats was a threat in disguise. Ratings from other branches did jobs completely different from their normal ones: with the ship stationery the Marine Engineers didn't have main engines to tend, so they set up desks in the heat of the outer deck to register the migrants as they appeared up the pilot ladder one by one; and Wardroom stewards abandoned their waiting and cleaning duties and prepared to offer bottled water and protein snacks to the new arrivals, hundreds of them at a time if need be. I normally started off by helping the stewards, until I knew if any of the migrants were newly-bereaved or particularly traumatised and needing – especially if they were from a Christian tradition – some pastoral contact and prayer.

I can remember on the night we had over 700 guests crammed on our Quarter Deck that I suppose was about 50'x50'. Several were tiny children, some of them with no clothes or possessions at all. We wore full PPE whenever we were amongst them to protect ourselves from diseases like scabies; and a young officer had taken a discarded glove, blown it up to make a five-fingered balloon, and given it to a little naked boy of about two. It was obviously his first ever toy, and his happiness was the last thing I expected to see amid such desperation.

I can understand why, at a time of difficult transformation of our civilian ministry in parishes, so many

---

[30] One is familiar with 'Hands to emergency stations'. This version was new to me; SOLAS means 'saving of lives at sea'.

of my colleagues are hunkering down in their current jobs. I can understand why the changing age-profile of our ministry – now normally a second career for middle-aged people – makes the pool of potential military chaplains much smaller than once it was. But if this lardy minister could swindle my way through Dartmouth in my early 40s, fire myself into that bunk towards 50, climb the ladder into the darkness of a sangar to visit Gurkhas thirty years younger than me, and stand on a roasting deck in the August Mediterranean sun and hand out water bottles to traumatised East African women when I was 54, might I suggest that even the more mature reader shouldn't skip over this chapter as if it couldn't possibly be asking you about a calling?[31]

A footnote to HERRICK.

On my return to Scotland I soon found my next parish ministry, in the Carse of Gowrie. One of the many guests at my induction service was Rev Scott Brown, by that time the new Chaplain of the Fleet, who in his previous role as the 'appointer' of chaplains had arranged my mobilised deployments. Another guest, of course, was my mother.

I invited to afternoon tea in my new manse those who were travelling a distance to attend the service that evening. Everyone seemed to be mixing nicely. And then I saw Scott, a tall and confident man usually, backed up against my dining room wall, with my middle-sized but sometimes quite intimidating mother practically poking him in the chest with the words 'Are you the young man who sent my daughter to Afghanistan?'

.

---

[31] The Church Offices would put you in touch with the Committee on Chaplains to HM Forces, and they would give you all the information and 'acquaint' visits you might need before you had to make any decisions.

My father's poem, mentioned on p120

There's a froth of gold in the west tonight
'Twixt purple and grey.
There's a ripple of red on the home land hills
And the call of a curlew softly thrills
While the mist creeps up from the Tay.

There's a drowsy stir in the Den tonight
Where small feet move.
There's a whisper of leaves in the holly's shade,
An owl floats over the dew-hung glade
And a silence falls on the grove.

There's a restless ache in my heart tonight
That will not be stilled
For it's sick that I am of this barren place,
Of the days that drag, of the years that race
Of the fond dreams unfulfilled.

But the homeland hills will sleep calm tonight
Nor share my pain,
For the power that I and the hills obey
Has settled my part in his mighty play
Nor opens his lips again.

With Sunny, Camp Souter Kabul, December 2010

SERMON FOR REMEMBRANCE DAY (READINGS: HEBREWS 9$^{24-28}$ AND MARK 12$^{38-44}$)

I wonder where your mind wanders during the silences we observe at Remembrance-tide. I wonder if it always goes to the same images and the same thoughts, to some iconic snapshot of trench-warfare, perhaps, or to the Whitehall Cenotaph, or to a mantlepiece picture of a smiling, nervous young face above World War Two battledress. I wonder too what comes to you along with the remembering, what the chief emotion is in those moments as you see our country normally share the distinctive traditions of this weekend. I mean, it has to be something more than remembering, doesn't it? Otherwise all we do is step through a door in time, wander around in some other place of our imagining, and step back into our world a little humbled perhaps but nothing more. What is that other thing, that feeling?

Is it a feeling of admiration? We have built a culture – a slightly false and rather embarrassing culture – of assuming our service personnel are all impressive, noble, admirable. Not close up they're not, I assure you, not all of them anyway. But I think we lionise them like that as an excuse for doing the same by extension to those who have been lost throughout modern history, and in turn we honour the lost with such admiration, I suspect, as a way of reducing the sense of waste and pointlessness of their deaths. As if it's almost all right to die young as long as you're a hero.

Is it for others a feeling not of admiration but of frustration? It makes me mad when people confuse Remembrance with political arguments about recent military history. We live in the kind of country in which the decision to deploy force is a political one, as it always and only should be; and those who are deployed – the ones we remember in these wistful days in November – are not to

blame for any of that and should only be remembered in love.

Or is the emotion of Remembrance one of patriotism? Is it an asking of the question whether our generation would be willing to give as much as our grandfathers gave for King and country, and our way of life (whatever that is), and our national values (whatever they are)? Are the glorious dead glorious only if they are our dead, and could there really be nothing glorious about an earnest, patriotic, family-loving, genuine, convinced member of the National Socialist Party or the Taliban? Might there be more integrity in an enemy motivated by conviction than in a British squaddie who almost certainly does not believe he is dying for King and country but rather dies for his mate being shot at in the same ditch? What is patriotic, truly?

So is it after all the emotion of regret? If you are not an out-and-out pacifist – and it's my personal belief that that option is available only to those whose jobs do not involve fixing the world's troubles – if you can conceive of war as a sad but unavoidable element of the past, present and future history of the planet, then regret will still arise whenever the wrong judgement call was made, whenever greater harm was done in the war than the harm that was meant to be prevented by it, whenever a little intervention sparked a great bloodbath, whenever an attempt at a just war was hijacked by evil or greedy figureheads. I entrust the decision to go to war only to a leader who is deeply capable of regret.

Truly I don't know what the right emotions are. Somehow, and differently in every one of our heads, there is a mixture of grief for millions of individuals killed in war, and a wrestling with the moral meaning of every armed conflict.

That moral meaning lies in the tension between the kind of self-sacrificial decision that results in your own death, and the kind of decisions some politicians and military leaders have to take that results in other people's deaths. And it's a huge moral range from the most immediate to the most geo-strategic. At the strategic end is a decision to send a Task Force to the South Atlantic with all that would eventually entail, or, let's say, a decision to help to overthrow a dictator in a North African country. Somewhere in the middle of the range is the decision to deploy that frigate in exactly that patch of water, or to send that battlegroup to Nar-e-Saraj in Helmand rather than somewhere more benign. And at the sharp end is the decision to steer this vehicle off this swept path in the Afghan desert to go and rescue those lads over there in that disabled ridgeback troop-carrier. In these life or death decisions the most powerful people make the decisions that have the biggest effects, but give least of themselves, while the people who have least say sacrifice everything.

Jesus watched the same thing happening in the temple treasury, where the people whose offerings kept that religious show on the road gave huge amounts that did not hurt their lifestyles in the slightest, but he honoured the poor widow whose mite paid for next to nothing and would not have been missed, but it cleaned her out, it cost her everything. Few would understand which was the more precious gift, precious at least in God's eyes; for humans have a very unimaginative way of deciding what has greatest worth. We are terribly interested in the importance of an *effect*, when all along God treasures the *intention* of the action. We read history written by the victors and succeeders and think it is the sole truth, while God loves the losers and the failures no less and remembers secret giving untold to the world.

All of which sets up the deepest truth of today's Bible readings. God is, we would tend to assume, at the grandest, most strategic, most cosmic end of that range of power, maker of all things and able by a sweep of divine will to change the course of history. Christ, who is God come into the world, is ruler of all things and worshipped by the very angels of heaven. They are beyond the most glittering and powerful and influential figures we can conjure into our minds' eyes. And yet. And yet. Christ behaved like the widow giving her tiny all, like the young squaddie throwing his life aside for a cause he could barely describe. Christ sacrificed himself, despite who he was himself, no, actually, *because* of who he was himself.

The writer to the Hebrews spells it out for us. In the old Jewish custom, year after year, priests would go into the Holy of Holies, the very middle chamber of the Jerusalem temple, and they would make sacrifices there, oxen and sheep and – for the poorest people – pigeons and such like. It was all done so that human beings wouldn't have to pay the price they really owed for their disobedience of God, the price of their own lives. There was a kind of double avoidance of that horrible reality: first, because priests would do the sacrificing and the worshipping in that moment in place of other people, and second, because livestock was used for the slaughter in place of those who actually owed the debt, deserved the punishment, whatever metaphor you like. Jesus Christ came and did it himself and gave himself; not paying some debt of his own because he uniquely didn't owe anything or deserve any punishment, and so doing what he did, giving what he gave, suffering what he suffered, because of his love for every one of us.

Are Christians particularly good at Remembrance and keen on it–as I rather think we are–because it reminds us of that central truth of our beliefs, undeserved suffering for an unselfish cause even to the extent of laying down one's life? Or is it the other way round, and Remembrance helps us to focus on a powerful and moving idea of individual sacrifice… which then reveals the significance of Jesus Christ to us in a new and forceful way?

So maybe, after all, that emotion I've been trying to identify, the right feeling to have in your heart during a

OH ALL RIGHT THEN

Remembrance day silence, is for Christian people a feeling of supplication, the longing and pleading contained in our prayers in every service.   We ask God to make of us whatever we are most fundamentally meant to be, to make us brave enough in faith to give up anything, sacrifice anything-up to and including ourselves-for the sake of a prize that is beyond this world, beyond the highest honour or respect or gratitude anyone could bestow, in peace or in war.

7 THE CARSE OF GOWRIE

The restructuring of the Church of Scotland's parishes and human resources is in process of changing my former charge out of my ability to recognise it any more. That's a good thing for my purpose, as my description of my ministry there can't possibly be a template for present or future ministers in the same place. The past tense in what follows is more than a courtesy; this really is a description of something that is no longer as it was even just a few years ago.

The charge that we short-handed as 'The Carse of Gowrie'[32] consisted of four historic places of worship run by three Kirk Sessions, and covered the area of five parishes if you had counted them any time between the eleventh century and the Wars of the Covenant.[33] There were larger

---

[32] I was always a bit uneasy with the term despite using it routinely myself, because there were two other charges that could perfectly reasonably have wanted to call themselves that too. Happily the presbytery boundary ran between me and both of them, so my impertinence didn't have to irk them on a daily basis.

[33] For parishioners there who are interested in the ecclesiastical arithmetic I'm using, I have added back in Rossie, which stopped being a separate parish in

church buildings in two larger villages, and smaller but very charming buildings in or near two hamlets. Regular attendance in my early years probably averaged, in the four buildings ordered by size, forty, thirty, twenty and ten, so a hundred on a Sunday morning in total.

Straight away you've spotted a challenge, and that is four pulpits in one morning. I inherited a lovely, warm and wise retired minister[34] who with precise correctness and thoughtfulness stayed in his part-time 'Assistant' post long enough to let me decide how I wanted to fill that billet, but took the initiative in resigning to allow it all to happen, much as I would have happily continued the working relationship. That gave us two churches each to serve in any week.

I had seen linked charges in other places, which often consisted of a larger congregation and a smaller one, and I guessed that the division of labour would be like that, with each preacher doing one of the villages 'doon the Carse' plus one of the little parishes 'up the Braes'. But no. The geography and the service times dictated otherwise, and so one week I'd be with the two larger congregations and the next I would be in the two tiny ones. It didn't take long for me to realise this was entirely the right way to arrange things; the 'feel' of worship in two congregations of similar size, and therefore the 'feel' of the materials I was preparing, had a consistency that made it easy.

Before I burrow deeper into the pattern of this period of ministry, let me tell the undignified story of the day I got the job.

In theory, you would think, a minister receives some spiritual indication of their calling, knows just exactly where they are meant to be, and therefore puts all their eggs into just one application to just one vacancy. In practice, of

---

the seventeenth century and was folded into Inchture. And of course Kinnaird had united its governance but not its building with Inchture more recently, giving my 5-4-3 taxonomy.

[34] Rev Robbie Donald

course, this does not work in the slightest. Only witness the fact that more than one person applies for each vacancy (well, normally), and you can see that the Holy Spirit does not allocate people to places quite as neatly as you might wish. So in practice, ministers apply for more than one charge simultaneously, and somehow have to wrestle in their hearts with the level of enthusiasm, commitment and calling they really feel as they sit in each interview. You really can't say 'there's no-one else, it's you I love', can you? Hey-ho.

I'd applied for two charges, and I'd already had the interview for the other one, which I'll call charge B. History will record that charge B ended up with a fabulous minister who is one of my favourite people, so please read this narrative in the light of that happy ending. My interview had gone pretty well, though, well enough that I'd take the job if it was my only offer at the end of the process. And yet, there was just a tiny sense of unease, of something not quite fitting; it certainly wasn't going to be a square peg in a round hole, but maybe a very slightly elliptical peg.

On a pleasant Sunday afternoon in January just a couple of weeks after my return from Kabul, I pitched up at Longforgan Church, the largest of the four in the Carse (charge A), to be interviewed by the Nominating Committee of the linked charge. And from the outset I felt like a round peg, the happiest possible fit. I was offered and accepted the nomination.

Something had happened ten minutes before the beginning of the interview, though, before I had even climbed out of my car parked outside the village shop. My mobile rang, and it was the convener of the Nominating Committee of charge B. They had voted to invite me to be their Nominee, but not quite unanimously; and they thought if I had another brief in-person conversation with them we might resolve the outstanding questions and reassure those who were doubtful. The conversation would need to be...

135

today. I indicated I could meet with them in the middle of the evening.

After the happy interview with Committee A, I had an indecently hasty meal with a very understanding elder who lived near the church, and then set off at haste for charge B. I do not wish to incriminate myself, so I will not describe in detail my driving; but I did get there just in time.

I allowed convener B to say an opening prayer, then I took a deep breath and explained my situation. Being very lovely people, they expressed some disappointment with the outcome and none with my handling of it. And, as I said, Providence was in fact smiling on them and had a much better plan for them than to give them me.

The moral of the story, and a truth I fervently believed even before that day: if you do not trust both the process and the unfolding of God's inscrutable will, don't enter a ministry with this as its system of parish appointments. What you need is the kind of open-mindedness I mentioned in the Introduction, and it's essential.

It's not only your mind that has to be open, but also your heart and personality. That's because in taking up a parish ministry it's not just an area of land, a set of buildings, a manse, and a diary-full of expectations that is delivered to you, but above all a large number of people.

To the neutral observer, some of the people will apparently receive from you more than they give, for they are the beneficiaries of your pastoral care, the next-of-kin of those whose funerals you conduct, the quiet presence in the Sunday pew who doesn't have particular duties within the congregation. To the same neutral observer, others of the people will apparently give to you more than they receive, for they are the people who visibly get things done.

I must say I think the neutral observer is often wrong. The 'receivers' of ministry, who often even themselves do not imagine they can possibly be offering you any value, are a deep source of blessing for the minister's spirit. Maybe it's my introverted personality, but I am energised by an hour spent with someone who is dying, and who has therefore shaken off the small talk that so often stands between a pastor and the conversation they wish they could have. I am moved by the person who secretly tells me that something I said on Sunday caused them to shed tears they had been needing rid of for months.

And it's equally wrong to think the obvious 'givers' are just giving. There is nothing like sharing the pain of a buildings emergency with a team of people to get to know them, spend time with them, drink coffee with them, and unwittingly create spaces for the opening up of conversation and understanding that maybe meets a need that had been hidden beneath the veneer of their competence.

But fair is fair, and you have to allow those endless givers to give in their own way, with their own style and flair, and sometimes with the unexpected outcomes that produces.

In my last Advent in the charge, the congregation of Inchture and Kinnaird – owner then of one of the larger and one of the smaller buildings – decided to have a Christmas fête complete with Nativity tableau. The fête element would be inside little Kinnaird Church; no surprise there, that was a December 'thing' of theirs. The tableau element, I was assured, would be on the 'playing field' outside[35], which I thought was a brave choice (in the *Yes, Minister* sense of 'brave') in a Perthshire winter with darkness by the back of 4 pm. And the cast of the tableau would be made up mainly of adults and most of them my senior office-bearers, so that was going to be interesting too.

On the evening before the great event, I popped up to Kinnaird to give that customary 'you're all doing very well' a minister gives to hard workers (I've changed reference

---

[35] Ministers get to be trustees *ex officio* of strange things like tiny sloping playing fields used as church car parks. The up side of these unsought appointments is that one's fellow trustees, often landed with the same job *ex officio* of some other role they play locally, are invariably delightful and interesting.

OH ALL RIGHT THEN

from *Yes, Minister* to *Are You Being Served*, but I'm confident you're all keeping up, thanks). Curiously, there were a number of animal pens round the Bethlehem stable under the temporary lighting. With my mind as open as I could make it I enquired what those were for, and was met with the matter-of-fact reply 'the alpacas'. I don't know about you, but I think alpacas come from South America; and I also think South America hadn't been discovered when Jesus was born in Judaea. But I'm sure alpacas would have loved to have been in the stable that night; wouldn't we all.

Back, though, to the serious business of providing services in four pulpits 52 times a year. To fill the vacancy in the part-time Assistant Minister post, I decided to try to be part of the Church's shift towards a much greater mix of types of preacher, and try to recruit a colleague who could identify, recruit and train worship leaders from within the very articulate and committed leadership of the congregations.

I found a once-in-a-lifetime colleague[36]: a scholar-pastor, an intellectual-encourager, a wordsmith-mentor. For three years she 'took the other two pulpits' every other week; but for most of the rest of her time she led study groups, *then* identified four people she knew were exactly what we needed, *then* trained them in theology, Biblical studies and conduct of worship. At the end of her three year appointment, we no longer needed an Assistant Minister, but had a team of four elders each taking a pair of services about once every six weeks, and amongst them (and alongside a locally-resident non-stipendiary 'auxiliary' minister and a smaller paid Assistantship[37]) filling the gaps left in our rota.

When I am scrolling social media in idle moments, I'm a sucker for little videos showing the progress of dogs rescued

---

[36] Nowadays properly referred to as Rev Professor Alison M Jack, Principal of New College

[37] Enthusiastically filled by Rev Alan Watt.

from their awful former lives, who are fostered to kind homes and eventually adopted. Often it's the fosterers who cave in and keep the dog for ever; that's known as a 'foster fail', which is a marvellously positive upending of the word 'fail'.

Well, we had a 'local worship leader fail', one of the four 'Carsies' (as those trainees became known and may still be for all I know). The process of training, the experience of leading worship, the taste of theological study, stirred a sense of vocation to ordained ministry in one of them.[38] It was hard to maintain the veneer of disappointment to be losing one of our assets in such a way.

Vestiges of the Carsies' training can be found now in the Worship Leaders Course offered from time to time through New College. In the crisis of funding and recruitment faced by our Church, and in the light of our experience in rural Perthshire, I suspect there is a fruitful pipeline our denomination needs to develop – or rather continue what has developed in various places including the one I've described. Just a thought.

Talking of worship…

They are hardy in the Carse of Gowrie, and not for them is an 11 a.m. start on a day as important as Easter Sunday – that would be for wimps. No, they like to climb something steep and then frighten the local wildlife with their Resurrection celebrations.[39]

There we were on top of a hill that really is called Tinkletap, beside Abernyte, standing in an empty sheep-field and being watched with great suspicion by the neighbouring field-full of farmed deer behind their very, very high fence. I had predictably stood with my back to

---

[38] Nowadays properly referred to as Rev Lorna Tunstall
[39] In Inchture they also liked the great outdoors in the week before Christmas, when they carol-sang (is that a word?) their way round one of the villages, inching their way towards a supper that beckoned singers with the irresistible prospect of cranberry-laced sausage rolls.

the east so that the congregation could face in that direction and get that sense of dawn and rising and all that. And then in the middle of a hymn, behind them all so they couldn't see what was snatching away all my attention, somewhere around Kinnoull Hill five miles to the west… a hot air balloon silently rose into the air and floated slowly away on the air-currents of the Carse. You couldn't have ordered that moment.

It was as far from 'routine' as you could imagine. Normally in a complex charge like the Carse, the effort and energy has to be spent in maintaining all the little elements of worship, administration, pastoral care, school chaplaincy and messy miscellany that make up the 'ordinary' week. I always likened it to the spinning of plates: not a small number of large plates but a large number of small plates. That is exhausting mentally, and even quite a well organised person can keep that up for only so long. One of the reasons I left that charge when I did was that I could feel myself flagging in exactly that task; that was no-one's fault locally.

And so my prayer for them is that in that area of the new Perth Presbytery, the re-shaping will pursue the same outcome we're trying to achieve in what we're doing in Orkney, so that many small tasks in governance, in elements of parish outreach, in communications, will be folded together into a much simpler pattern and give all the clergy and elders some breathing space and time to think about bigger things, not least the things that inspire worship.

I think buildings inspire worship. Elsewhere I have railed against the powerful forces in the Church that have accepted and promoted a highly functional standard for judging buildings.[40] I need the kind of space that *of its nature* shuts me up and gives my inner being some peace and quiet.

---

[40] Visions and Authorities, chapter 1.

OH ALL RIGHT THEN

It need not be ancient; it need not be impractical; but it needs to be the kind of space that makes me think 'here I am'. Does that make sense?

And it is in the non-routine development of our buildings, to be whatever it is we each need them to be, that we probably lean most heavily on that even greater asset, the best of our people. Many ministers have war stories of refurbishments of buildings. I'm torn between thinking that no minister should ever have to do it twice, and thinking every minister ought to do it twice because they would be able to bring so much knowledge to the second project learned the hard way from the first.

In Inchture Church during the first five years of my ministry there (and they'd been at it for a while before that) a group of office-bearers poured hundreds and hundreds of hours[41] into a £560,000 project to maintain the exterior of the building and start to transform the interior space for its twenty-first century use. I won't bore you with the details of someone else's beloved building. Remember, though, what I said about the greatest givers often receiving far more than others might notice? For all of us, some of the happiest memories of that project are of those evenings spent in front of the fire in the lounge-bar of the local hotel, as we wrestled with a feasibility study or searched online for another grant-making body or heard our Convener break to us the news of yet another historical obstacle.

Our church building was the latest in a series of churches on that spot stretching back to the late Middle Ages, and the fact that its many layers of foundations were an archaeologist's dream meant that they were a bit of a refurbisher's nightmare. You might imagine the architectural adaptability required to redesign some of the larger cupboards so that they would go round and not through traces of a medieval wall. And perhaps you will sympathise with me when I tell you that I answered the

---

[41] The individual who-everyone there knows-poured 90% of that effort in, would not want to be named in a book like this, which kind of says it all.

manse phone one lovely June day in 2016 not long after the work had begun, to hear a new voice say 'How do you do, Dr MacLean. We haven't met but I'm your architect's retained archaeologist and I'm phoning you from your church. Do you have time to come along?' I didn't know we even had a 'retained archaeologist', and I sensed that I had just been alerted to something that would be as expensive as it would be interesting.[42]

I'll limit what I describe here, since it did have a pastoral (albeit very historic) element to it. But with the very gracious permission of those most personally affected, what we found has been displayed in photographic form in the church's (new!) meeting room, so without breaching confidences I can say it involved coffins, old, splendid, lead coffins.

New College did not prepare me for that.

I can remember the time when, as a matter of principle and some pride, churches were locked between one Sunday and the next, the point being that when the congregation left at the end of their Sunday service they were taking the work of the Church into the world of their weekday lives and it was important not to imagine that the Spirit of the Church somehow remained within those four walls for the other six days.

Throughout my ministry, and at an accelerating pace I think, the philosophy has changed, and our churches are increasingly meant to be multi-functional spaces that are comfortable, resourced, safe, warm, flexible, busy. As I said earlier, I think you can get that wrong in a baby-with-bathwater kind of way, by losing the numinous in a dash for the functional.

In the Carse during my ministry, I think they had a lovely mixture of buildings that complemented each other and the overall mission of their congregations beautifully – which I

---

[42] The additional cost of what they'd found that day was less than my annual stipend but not much.

hope tells you that sometimes those four communities knew to work as one when the sanctuary of one group was perfect for some event created for everyone: a concert, a sale, a wedding.

In Kinnaird Church, they had sales afternoons down to a fine art. In their small , rectangular, two-aisled building, they steered their patrons through the little vestibule (buy your tickets), up one aisle with plywood boards covering the pews on either side and covered with the merchandise of local artists, across in front of the platform on which the communion table had been replaced by the baking stall (J's chocolate cake, oh man I can still taste it), down the other aisle towards the vestry/kitchen from which the refreshments were being served, and back out into the kirkyard.

In Abernyte Church, which I will go to my grave arguing is the most beautiful building in Perthshire, they would occasionally find passing cyclists pause, visit their cruciform gem with its gorgeous internal roof and indescribable late afternoon light, and instantly decide they had to hold their wedding there.

In Longforgan Church, you knew you were standing on a spot that traced the very history of the Church in that area back to its roots with St Modwenna before the first millennium. And yet in the current building your eye was caught by a funeral slab of a passing knight, or by Stephen Adams' 'Abraham' window, while your ear was soothed by the charming two-manual 1924 Compton organ.

And then in Inchture Church, when the dust had literally settled and the scaffolding removed, and the lift commissioned, and the water-heater installed in the swanky new kitchen, they had space to hire, room for a monthly Folk Evening, and somewhere comfortable for the children to go during the service without crossing a dangerous road to a different building.

OH ALL RIGHT THEN

I'd been there no more than about a month when I realised that I could have been transported blindfolded into any of the buildings, and I would just feel which one I was in.

No evening would ever be long enough for a parish minister to describe their work, their world, their people, their challenges. For most of them most of the time, they will find the routine and rhythm of 'normal' time is the easy bit, and the time of change and transformation, of special opportunity, is the draining and demanding part of their ministry. For some of us some of the time, though, as I found in the Carse, those tiny spinning plates[43] on their wobbly sticks are what is most wearing, and it is in the moment when someone you can trust says to the refurbishment group 'it's gonnae happen', and you all dare to dare, that it can seem like the most obvious thing in the world to do even while it makes your tummy flip with nerves.

One more thing, and here is a good place to say it. Don't forget that the minister might be a 'receiver' or a 'giver' at different moments throughout their ministry. 2016 in my head is not, first and foremost, the year of the Inchture refurbishment; it is the year in which I lost both my parents within a fortnight. This book is not about that. Those congregations cleared for me the little bit of life's path that I walked then: they allowed me time, and they chose not to notice the things that wavered, and they adapted to things I was less able to manage for a while, and they didn't count too closely the amount of time I took for house-emptying. In the simplest and most human of ways they ministered to their minister; congregations usually do.

---

[43] By that I mean the round of repeating administrative tasks, which may have to be triplicated across three linked parishes; or maybe the mix from week to week of pastoral cases requiring one's emotional intelligence to be deployed very differently in the different situations.

OH ALL RIGHT THEN

As you know if you've kept the time-line of this book in your mind, it was in August 2016 that I spent that month on the migrant rescue work in the Mediterranean with HMS ENTERPRISE. Personal communications were very limited, and the chance to catch up with one's e-mail was patchy. It might be a few days since the last round-up of the inbox, and it was exciting to scan the message headings to see who had been in touch, and whether I needed to know anything pastoral about any of the parishes back home. The buildings project was progressing after the set-back of June, with more predicable things like scaffolding and pointing and engineering well under way. One day, somewhere just north of the limit of Libyan territorial waters, I found myself looking helplessly at an email that was entitled 'Another Coffin'. What was I supposed to…

Inchture Church, full of curiosities

SERMON FOR X'S INDUCTION AROUND ALL SAINTS

What a marvellous week to begin a new ministry; the week of All Saints Day. The last big event in our Christian year before we think of approaching Advent again, All Saints Day, 1st November, neatly lands on Sunday this year, as a kind of gift to you, X.

At All Saints the Church celebrates that she is the community of the faithful, of the sanctified, of the saved. It's a time when maybe we get to be just a little mystical about ourselves, and imagine that there is after all some kind of holiness about us that we don't think about most of the time. We celebrate ourselves as the community of those who would be faithful, people in the middle of doing our level best to be who God asks us to be. We celebrate ourselves as the community of those allowing ourselves the adventure of following in Christ's way, men and women and children who are just brave enough to ask God to make the big decisions for us and see where we end up. We celebrate ourselves as the community of those who are living out the story, and it is a story that begins in the pages of the Bible with God's love come to earth and continues in and through us until all is done and we have played our part. Because we are Protestants, we celebrate ourselves as the sanctified not the celebrated, as the faithful not the famous, as saints without the capital 'S'; but it still counts.

St Paul writing to the Romans described the process of becoming saints:

For if while we were enemies, we were reconciled to God through the death of his Son, much more surely having been reconciled, will we be saved by his life.

At All Saints we go beyond the bad habit of Western Christianity – which is a kind of accident of early church history – of stopping half way through that verse, of thinking of our salvation as just being about the forgiveness of our sin and the healing of our weakness by Christ's death, as if the best we could ever do would be to end up the way we started before we started fouling it all up. No, when we think of ourselves as saints, I think we behave more like the Eastern Churches, where people are taught to find their salvation in their sharing of Christ's life, growing more and more close to God, more and more like God with every passing year and every passing prayer. Reconciled by Christ's death, yes, and saved by Christ's life. It's less about tidying ourselves up after making a mess of things, and more about having a gloriously untidy but increasingly intimate connection with the divine, and discovering that to be the greatest thing of all.

X has come to this place to encourage this people to be the saints they are called to be, without embarrassment at such an elevated idea, without false modesty to get in the way of having a go at holiness.

All Saints Day is propped up in the Christian calendar by two pillars, the days on either side of it. Saturday is, of course, Hallowe'en, which stands to All Saints Day exactly as Christmas Eve stands to Christmas Day ('hallow' and 'saint' are the same idea from different language roots). At Hallowe'en, helped especially by the children in our lives, we deal with everything that most frightens us in life by making fun of it, and we do it so well that big business has paid us the compliment of commercialising it and turning it into a shopping season. We laugh then at death, at threat, at the things beyond sight that make us nervous, at everything we cannot humanly control. We dress it up in skeleton outfits or ghostly sheets, rather than think about the actual terror of losing a loved one or having to face our own ending or a beginning in a life beyond this one that we haven't quite sorted out in our heads.

But in every day of life the Church faithfully wrestles with a much wider variety of evils, seen and unseen. With every pastoral visit to the bereaved and every prayer said in the quietness of a home darkened by loss, with every admission of a new resident to one of the Church's care homes or rehabilitation units to bring safety and security to a fragile life in Christ's name, with every word of prophecy spoken out by the Church in countries where genocide or slavery or female genital mutilation or gang warfare permeates society, with every evening spent working with a youth organisation in this community that keeps teenagers safe from their worst temptations, and my list could go on… Christ's Church does Christ's work to hallow not just each of us as individuals but the imperfect world in which we live and serve.

X, in his/her preaching and leading, will arouse your passions as the people of God, the saints of this place, to do work that will extend far beyond these walls.

And then on Monday we will reach the least celebrated of the trio of festivals, All Souls. It's a slightly redundant festival in our Reformed tradition because we do not have a practice of praying for the souls of the dead – our theology doesn't require it. But it's worth pausing to realise that for two thousand years people a lot like us, some of them related to us by blood, have blundered their way to sainthood, and been surprised and bashful about their calling, and made a Horlicks of their relationships, and been restored only by God's grace, and poured their love and resources into churches like this, and completed their earthly lives, and handed on their baton, and finished their race, and grown closer to God and more like God indeed, and maybe left a few footprints into which we can fit our toes, our little steps behind them. Their significance stretches forward far beyond the moment of their deaths to influence our religion, and we realise our significance somehow stretches back to them as we care for the assets and traditions and worship of this place and community left to us by them. We hold hands with all souls as we realise that our Christian life extends far beyond the span of our years in this world; we are part of something so much bigger that it can take away those biggest fears.

X will show you the vast space you occupy, the grandeur of your unlimited life.

Remember that picture of himself that Jesus painted, sent by God into the world to gather us up, to gather up everything and leave nothing behind. As minister and people together, hanging on to that promise and comfort through thick and thin, you will prove yourselves to be saints of the Church, you will triumph over the whole world, you will take your place with dignity in the history of God's presence in this community, and you will grow closer to God who made and makes you, who saved and redeems you, who leads and liberates you. For this congregation of the saints, for its new ministry, for all who love and pray for it,

Thanks be to God.

8 MISCELLANEOUS THOUGHTS (SOME DEEP)

Ministry is always **messy**, with little bits and pieces that don't quite fit into the large categories like 'pastoral' or 'governance' or 'worship'. This penultimate chapter offers a couple of those outlying kinds of experience, amongst the hundreds of such pieces of flotsam and jetsam other ministers would describe to you out of their all-different lives.

And ministry is always **imperfect** because we are imperfect, and we leave behind us a trail of sometimes slightly disappointed or sometimes deeply hurt people we were trying to love but got it wrong. So the other thing this chapter does is warn would-be or new ministers what big mistakes of mine to be sure to avoid – without (I hope) being indulgently breast-beating about them.

CHAPLAIN TO THE MODERATOR OF THE GENERAL ASSEMBLY

After Covid knocked the General Assembly right out of the park in May 2020, an on-line Assembly was arranged for 2021, and the elder designated to be its Moderator was Lord

Wallace of Tankerness, Jim Wallace. The Moderator has two chaplains of his or her own choosing, and Jim chose his parish minister at the time[44] and me to support him and Rosie.

Normally the chaplains act as *aides de camp* to the moderatorial party, administrative assistants to the Moderator during the Assembly itself, spiritual supporters in personal devotions during the week, and bringers of jollity and energy to the various social occasions that are sprinkled through that third week of May. To a crashing introvert like me, but with my history with the Assembly, the first three tasks were meat and drink while the last would have made my heart sink. 2021 had virtually no people present and therefore no parties, and suited me perfectly.

The Lord High Commissioner that year, representing The Queen for the week, was the Earl of Strathearn (otherwise then known as the Duke of Cambridge, who is now the Prince of Wales). Rather than attend an empty Assembly Hall each day (as a Lord High Commissioner would do in normal times), he attended only the opening and closing sessions, and used the rest of the week to undertake a fuller-than-usual programme of visits to church projects and other initiatives around Scotland.

At the closing session he brought the Countess of Strathearn with him, her only visit to the Hall during the week. In normal times three members of the Assembly meet 'Their Graces' at the entrance archway of New College Quad to welcome them to the event; but of course we didn't have three members of the Assembly to hand. So this chaplain was going to have to do it; fair enough.

CrossReach, the Church's wonderful social care agency, had been producing face-masks in the Church's own tartan, and it had been decided that I would present Their Graces with two of them as I greeted them; but at this point of

---

[44] Rev Fraser Macnaughton

Covid hygiene measures we were still avoiding passing things to each other by hand. We tried setting up a little table beside me on the pavement; it just didn't look right. But as chance would have it, I had (in my other capacity as Convener of the Committee on Chaplains to Her Majesty's Forces) delivered my Report that morning, an occasion attended-in a normal year–by military chaplains in Number 1 uniform. And one of the very few people in the building, a member of the Assembly Business Committee[45], had sportingly turned up for that day in his uniform as an Army Reserve chaplain. Chaplains, especially retired ones, do not often issue orders; but I did.

We found a large offering dish, plonked the face-masks on it, and poor Mike stood to attention holding a heavy weight in front of him for about fifteen minutes while we waited for the numberplateless[46] car to arrive. It is a wonder to me that he didn't fall forwards onto his nose.

When I explained the provenance of the masks to Their Graces, Prince William looked at them with a slightly uncertain smile, waiting for me to hand one to him. 'I'm sorry, Sir', I had to say, 'I'm not supposed to hand them to you, do you mind just picking them up yourself?'…. 'Oh, of course!'

Never let anyone persuade you that being a minister can't ever be utterly memorable fun.

BROADCASTING
Depending on what your natural skills happen to be, people will approach you to do some fascinating things, and few are more interesting and entertaining than broadcasting. Whether it's a *Thought for the Day* on a local or regional radio station, or the pre-recorded early morning *Prayer for the Day* on Radio 4 (you soon find out who your local farmers are,

---

[45] Rev Michael Mair, who has recovered sufficiently to become a distinguished Convener of the Assembly's Business Committee, which just shows you the resilience of our Army Reservists.
[46] Remember Chapter 4!

as only they ever hear it), the challenge is to say something to engage an audience more diverse than any that ever sits in front of you in church, and to do it in a fraction of the number of words available for a sermon.

Occasionally I am asked to 'do' the mid-morning Radio 4 LW *Daily Service* from The Tun in Edinburgh on a Friday. This service uses existing recordings of hymns, and the spoken parts of the service are recorded earlier on the same morning, edited to length, and spliced with the hymns to create a programme just short of fifteen minutes. However, the continuity announcements between programmes sometimes vary just a little in length, and the point at which the service recording begins to play therefore varies a little too. That's a problem with a sound-file with its length now fixed, because the end of the programme should come a second or two before the 10 o'clock pips, without either leaving a yawning gap or committing the capital BBC offence of 'crashing' the time signal.

So the one thing I neither write in advance, nor record, is the final blessing at the end of the service. Once the programme has begun to broadcast, the producer now knows precisely how many seconds will elapse between the end of the recording and the beginning of the pips, and tells me 'we need a final blessing that lasts 22 seconds', or whatever; and I then have about fourteen minutes to write that, and then broadcast live for just that tiny snippet of prose at the very end of everything. 'Amen. *(silent one potato two potato)* Peep, peep…'

You think that sounds a bit odd? During lockdown, we did it all from home with everything prerecorded. That didn't used to be a thing because of the terrible sound quality on the landline phones which were all we had, remember? Meeting apps now allow near-broadcast quality sound to be sent by almost anyone. Near but not quite; and it's much better when you're recording in a space that muffles all resonance (as a studio does). And where is that space in any given home? *Under your duvet.* So please

OH ALL RIGHT THEN

imagine most of the external contributors to the radio programmes you love, sitting cross-legged on their bed, sweltering fully-clothed under their duvet, earnestly debating politics… or even preaching the Gospel.

CONVENING GENERAL ASSEMBLY COMMITTEES

I have written[47] of the distinction between the staff of 121 and the voting members of its various trusts and committees; both groups contain ministers, deacons and elders but the roles are very different between those who are more like civil servants and those who are a little more like political decision-makers. It is a different set of challenges again to be asked to lead one of those bodies as its Convener.[48] During the year you will chair its meetings, co-ordinate the work of its members, defend its work or role or budget in the constant cut and thrust of internal Church politics, or represent its views through the media when something thrusts your agency into the public eye. At the Assembly, you present its annual Report and deal appropriately (on a range from warm welcome to die-in-a-ditch resistance) with proposals coming from the floor during the debate.

In 2013 I was asked to convene one of the large committees inside what was then known as the Ministries Council. I was not already a member of the Education and Support Committee, but it was one that all ministers knew well because it dealt with recruitment/selection/training for the ministry, as well as the pastoral care of ministers in times of illness, bereavement and so on. I was happy to be parachuted in to its chair.

I proudly told my slightly deaf mother of my appointment. 'What a very good and creative idea that is', she commented, puzzlingly. 'You think it's a 'creative' idea

---

[47] see Visions and Authorities chapter 2A
[48] In the Church of Scotland we retain some old Scottish linguistic conventions, and perhaps the most noticeable of these is our spelling of 'Convener'.

of the Church to appoint me as a committee convener?', I asked, every so slightly defensively. 'No, no, no', said Mother, 'I think it's super to get ministers to do sport; so many of them look unfit.'

THINGS YOU NEED TO DO BETTER THAN I DID

Hundreds of things, I'm sure; just ask anyone except me and they will produce the list of my failings that you need to avoid. Two things, though, seem to me to matter most.

First, sort yourself out – now, not decades hence – in terms of the interior life, the pattern and discipline of personal prayer, the development of the awareness of the soul beneath and within, the exercise of the desire for connection with God. And I do mean 'desire for' and not 'achievement of'; Lord knows how few ministers we would be left with if we required them to think they'd cracked this stuff.

Use the help the Church gives its ministers to hire a trusted Spiritual Director and, whatever he or she guides you to do, make that activity the first priority of all your time management.

And don't allow yourself the apparently virtuous cop-out of praying entirely for other people and not for yourself. Most of what you need is known only to you; so even those who love you enough to pray for you are not going to be able to open up that can of worms, and you need to be doing that praying all by yourself.

A few years ago, at my first ever meeting with a Spiritual Director, she told me pretty much what I wrote in that last paragraph. I pushed back slightly piously, telling her that as a parish minister I surely ought to be praying for the people in my care. B tutted and said, 'If you must, write their names on a piece of paper, place a lighted candle on top of it, commend them all to God… and then get on and pray about you.' I don't quite do that, but it's amazing how easy it is to create an Alexa routine that breaks a Quiet Time up into little chunks with wee bell noises, creating time for supplication and time for intercession.

Second, work out your theory of Theological Anthropology and apply it to yourself. What do I mean?

What is a human being? What makes up a thinking, feeling, relational, reflective, spiritual entity? (Anthropology) What would we say differently, if anything, when we regard that entity from the point of view of the Divine, of a Creator, of a Redeemer, of a companioning Spirit? What is the destiny of that human when the landscape is not just of this world but involves the whole economy of God's eternal plans? (Theoretical Theological Anthropology, if I may coin a phrase) What does all of that mean for the particular life I am leading: whether the critical variable is that I am an astronaut, or a wife, or an MS sufferer, or a local councillor, or an inhabitant of a low-lying often-flooded Pacific island. Or a Church of Scotland minister. (Applied Theological Anthropology)

If you become a minister, *work out who and how you will be*. Come to terms with your politics, and whether and when they belong in your ministry; with your sexuality, and how fully you intend to live a personal life; with your family's routine, and whether you are going to allow a congregation to expect anything of anyone else you bring with you to their manse; with your passions and commitments and hobbies, and how private you need your non-working days to be each week. And much more.

The Church has often debated whether ordination alters your personal identity or only (only!) your life's work. In a higher catholic tradition, clergy are sometimes treated as having different expectations upon them as people (clerical celibacy being an obvious example). In a lower tradition (eg Brethren) there is no category distinction like that, though certain leaders might earn great respect. In our Reformed type of Church, we are somewhere in between, entrusting some important tasks to our ministers (Sacramental ministry, and the regular blessing of the people, for instance), but not regarding them as a distinct class of persons.

Therefore, when you are answering those identity questions – and not leaving some of them for thirty years, trust me – I would commend that 'middle' style of Theological Anthropology. Be the person you would have been if this pesky suspicion of a calling hadn't disrupted your life; and then find the way of combining the privilege of ministry with the blessing of being just another beloved child of God.

THE 95:85 RULE

There are places in which the most significant thoughts get thunk. In the Introduction I showed you Yesnaby, for example. Another thinking-place in Orkney, if you can manage to find it when it's empty, is the Italian Chapel which I'll describe to you in the next and final chapter. And it was while I was spending a little bit of time in silence there years ago that a rule popped into my head without any apparent train of thought leading up to it. So, assuming it must have come from a pretty good source, I'm going to share it with you, and I don't think it matters whether you are a minister or not.

Do not demand of yourself that you get everything right all the time. If you do, on the first time you fail you will forever have fallen short of 100%, and then you'll just beat yourself up and achieve less than you still could. Ask of yourself an average of 95% in competence, kindness, memory, effort, understanding, everything. Notice when you managed that, or when you knew you were going to have to average it over a few days (like saying 'best of three' when you lose a coin toss)!

Demand of everyone else... *85%*. Don't let yourself become annoyed with someone until they've run through a big allowance of your patience, because you don't know what's troubling them today or what they've never owned up they found hard to do. You will still have boundaries in your dealings with them; you will still need them to step up to tasks that can't be left undone.

I have liked myself better since I stopped being unkind in my expectations of myself. And who knows, perhaps other people like me more since I began to give them more of a break than I give me.[49]

There, that's my gift to you.

HAS THIS HELPED?

I have no idea whether this collection of daft tales and lifelong ponderings will be helpful to those who read it. If you belong in the first target readership, and have wondered about the possibility of calling to ministry, there is an awful lot more you could discover than the arbitrary selection of experiences I have been trying to bring to life for you. On the Church's web-site, in a feature called 'Talking Ministry', you will find monthly articles by ministers and deacons, sharing their own journeys and the distinctive features of the way they are serving. Read all of them, and realise your head is being expanded far further than it was by reading this book.

If you belong in the other target population, of those who give thanks for the ministry of the Church they love, but might have been a little hazy about the stuff that makes up a minister's calling, I hope I have given you reason for celebration, and perhaps some hints about the kind of support (no, not sport, don't do that to him or her) you can give to the minister who cares for you.

---

[49] One consequence of moving from one place to another during a lifetime of ministry is that the people who worked with you thirty years ago no longer do. Goodness knows how surprised many of them would be to discover what the older, wiser, calmer version of their scratchy younger colleague looks like.

OH ALL RIGHT THEN

To finish with (after a final sermon) one more chapter, and it's a road trip. So buckle up...

With Adjutant on a Humanitarian Assistance Drop
Kabul, 2010

SERMON AFTER EASTER 2024 (READING FROM I JOHN 3)

There are several statements in that reading from John's letter that make me pretty uncomfortable: stuff about God being revealed and turning out to be a lot like me, stuff about my transformation to be one of the children of God... and the transformation being already, in the past. If that sort of language doesn't make you feel rather inadequate too, then I think we need to swap places, and good luck to you.

Let's face it, we are much happier listening to stories about holy people displaying understandable human virtues: tales of bravery, heart-warming narratives about love, inspiring histories of justice done for the poor in the face of the wicked rich. Christianity as basic moral teaching to individuals and communities is something we can cope with in our heads.

It's this more mystical kind of writing, that talks about encounter and connection between you and an actual God, about the life of your immortal and therefore eternal soul, about your faith meaning something substantial happening deep inside you, *that* is what is very much more alarming. And that, I think, is the difference between conscious Christian commitment and what's known as cultural Christianity.

Cultural Christianity is a phrase that describes the way elements of Christianity are scattered about in our culture. Our local football teams are drawn from the parishes that once identified everyone's church membership; that's cultural Christianity. People with no religious belief come to funeral services in church, and don't object when I say religious things, because they're used to funerals being like that; that's cultural Christianity. Rightly or wrongly, my friend Graham sits in the House of Lords as a Church of England bishop; that's cultural Christianity. In the last two cases, the Church has the opportunity to do great good as a result of those things, they give us a place to raise our voice and declare God's love, but people bump into those things regardless whether they would say they were committed believers.

I think those words in the first letter of John are addressed to those of us whose faith goes deeper than cultural Christianity, for whom finding bits of religious history scattered around our community doesn't fully describe what that religion means in our lives, who look inwards to the space where we think and pray, and know it is a place where we encounter something more, *or at least we yearn to encounter something more and we try to be open to that.*

Whether the writer of this letter dreamed they would be addressing people two thousand years down the path of Christian history I do not know. But addressed we are, as those people – perhaps these days those relatively few people – who really do want to drink deeper waters, plum inner depths, encounter the unfiltered God. If you are willing for *that* to be who *you* are, you are already brave.

The first two verses of our reading say this:

See what love the Father has given us, that we should be called children of God; and that is what we are. The reason the world does not know us is that it did not know him. Beloved, we are God's children now; what we will be has not yet been revealed. What we do know is this: when he is revealed, we will be like him, for we will see him as he is.

The first lesson I notice in those challenging sentences, is that one day we are going to discover how much like God we are. We should have known that all along of course: Genesis talks about God deliberately making humankind in the divine image, and Christ was both human and divine without having to be split down the middle. God and the human are not as different as we sometimes imagine.

Gosh I'm sure there is no end to the things you can deduce from that rather startling statement, that you are an awful lot like God even if you can't quite believe it yet until you see it with your own eyes one day.

OH ALL RIGHT THEN

For one thing, it might make it easier for you to pray, because if you imagine you are speaking to someone who can easily hear you, totally understand you, already know you, you will stop parroting the formulae of prayer you think you ought to use and start just saying what you think and feel as you would to the most trusted friend you've ever had.

For another thing, it means you have the ability to do the extraordinary things that go beyond normal human virtue: you have the power to forgive those other people will not forgive; you have the power to face death without the normal human fear of it; you have the power to be the agent of the kind of transforming peace that Jesus said the world just wasn't capable of giving.

You are like God and not by accident. It is, if you like, your superpower. It is also, admittedly, pretty daunting.

The second lesson in these verses for me is the idea that we are *already* the children of God, and that tells me two home truths.

The first is that in some sense some transformation is complete, the process of adoption has been done, I'm not still waiting. Now of course that's rather at odds with all the bits of the New Testament that talk of a transformation still to happen, and God knows there is a lot of me that needs thorough transformation – I am a misshapen and sinful soul and lots of bits need fixed. But just as doting parents see their disabled child as utterly perfect, there is a sense in which *all that I imperfectly am is whom God loves without qualification.*

The second home truth about my adoption is that it wasn't my idea. The Christian Church has been great at preaching the prevenient love of God – prevenient meaning it comes first. The Christian Church has also been a little too good at preaching the need for human decision about faith, or the Church's condemnation of people for very worldly reasons.

But while I'm setting up the structures of my religious judgement, Christ is standing at my shoulder politely clearing his throat... and waiting for me to look up and realise that in truth he and I are way past that stage, and I am sitting within the company of the family of God whether I like it or not and always have been. So no-one gets to condemn me.

There's one more idea that intrigues me in those two intense verses: the world does not know us because it does not know him.

I spoke of cultural Christianity and contrasted it with something rather more intentional, rather more interior, rather more prayerful perhaps.

I think I want to take another step and say that *sometimes* we find we are being *counter*-cultural, working against even some of the apparently most respectable assumptions society makes. I say 'sometimes'; obviously it's not our job to trash and ignore perfectly good universal human virtues like respect for property or the pursuit of democracy. Sometimes, though, it is our job to remember how Jesus offended respectable people, and reprise that in our day and age.

I've already mentioned that kind of behaviour, when we forgive because God does, even when other people can't. Let me take that further to show what it would look like as a revolutionary idea.

We have a system of international law that allows nations to wield retributive justice on each other when they come under attack. There's the kind of action that prevents further attack, there's the kind of justice that demands reparation for damaged buildings. Retributive justice is the kind of justice that is simply punishment; and international law says it's OK as long as it's proportionate – it's known as the *lex talionis*. Obviously a lot of the debate about Gaza is about whether Israel's actions have been proportionate in that kind of way.

What, though, if the worldwide Church were to argue against retributive justice entirely, from that position of radical forgiveness that we know is God's loving nature?

OH ALL RIGHT THEN

Let Israel genuinely defend itself against further attack, yes, let the international structures of justice deal with Hamas and free the hostages, yes, establish a method to rebuild the cities that have been destroyed, yes, give new loving homes and education to the children, yes. But what if we all called for an end to all retribution, tit-for-tat, eye-for-eye? How many lives would that have saved in Palestine, and how big a revolution in the world's way of measuring out just deserts would that create?

That is one example of Christianity as revolutionary, world-changing, as revealing what God is really like by being like that ourselves. I could give other examples: of radical inclusion of minorities along with majorities, of being guided by the wisdom of the people we normally least listen to, of being stewards of creation instead of its masters. You could give examples of still other things I haven't thought to dream of.

John's point is that in all of these things society around us may find us strange and awkward and downright inconvenient in our words and our attitudes. That is what John means about the world not understanding us because it does not understand God. Does that sound like a calling you could embrace? That, too, would be brave.

For everything in you that shows me what God is like, Thanks be to God.

9 SRB AND HW

For this final chapter let me do something different. I won't reflect further on parish ministry, since we've shared lots of that already in Chapters 3 and 7. And I certainly don't want to tell any stories from my current ministry, as I'd like to stay there for a bit longer please.

So let me take you on a journey in my car, one that I make about once a month from my home in the village of St Margaret's Hope to another homely space in the village of Longhope. It's 33 miles of driving plus 35 minutes on a ferry, each way.

If I explain the purpose of the trip you'll learn about the changing shape and intensity of ministry in a Church undergoing alarming restructuring of assets and jobs.

Here in Orkney, we have had to find ways to serve the whole community of these islands in the coming years with slightly more than half the amount of paid ministry we used to be entitled to support from the Church's national stipend fund. Being entitled to pay a stipend is not the same thing as succeeding in recruiting the ministers to receive it, and so we have been working for yonks with some unfilled posts (vacancies, to use the technical term). Most ministers have been moderating (ie chairing) the Kirk Sessions of those vacant parishes, which is known as acting as 'Interim Moderator'. It is quite common, therefore, to be minister of one place and Interim Moderator of another.

Our restructuring will bring us together into a single team with a shared responsibility for Orkney; that will get rid of vacancies, technically speaking, and certainly of interim moderatorships. However, we'll keep a recognisable 'geographical' element in our individual ministries, by giving members of the team pastoral care for the area where they live and also for somewhere that has no resident minister. And, hands up, yes, that will in practice give quite a continuity from the old system for day-to-day work, though not so much for the governance bit (which is the real point).

For me that will certainly mean still caring for South Ronaldsay and Burray (the SRB of the mysterious chapter heading) because it's where I live. It is likely that I will also have care of the biggest land mass outside Orkney's Mainland, which is the beautiful and much-visited island of Hoy and Walls (that's the HW). And so, as we prepare for the change, I have already taken on the interim moderatorship (under the old system) of HW, in the hope of giving them a smooth transition to the new structure without a sudden change of face. I hope that makes sense to any bewildered Anglicans, Catholics or Baptists trying to make head or tail of all this.

About once a month I spend a weekend over there, in the village of Longhope and the house called Kirkside. You encountered it, and its local fire brigade, earlier in the book. Now you understand what I was doing there. It serves both as accommodation for preachers and as our Sunday worship space; and my two night stay there always feels like a bit of an adventure and a profoundly different way of doing ministry.

OH ALL RIGHT THEN

The journey starts in South Ronaldsay at lunch-time on a Saturday, so that I can catch the 2.15 ferry from Houton (a little harbour on the North shore of Scapa Flow) to Lyness (a harbour on the East coast of Hoy and Walls, in North Walls to be exact, where Britain had one of its biggest naval bases during the War). I used to take a later boat to get me to Kirkside at tea-time, but I would be just too tight to catch the one shop that serves the community, which consequently necessitated a detour to Kirkwall's Tesco *en route* for provisions, which always felt like a nuisance. So I've taken to travelling a little earlier and a little easier, and buying my bits and pieces of food at Groats' shop.

Back to the starting-point though. South Ronaldsay is a contender for the birthplace of Christianity in the heart of Orkney. The other serious contender is Papa Westray, as each can boast an early medieval mission arriving on their shores and planting the Gospel's seed. I probably have to concede greater antiquity to Papay's tradition; but we in SR are closer to Kirkwall, the county town, and perhaps would have had stronger connections to civic life in the middle of Orcadian society way back then.

Anyhow, it wasn't so much a seed that was planted here as a pair of feet. Drive down to the southernmost tip of South Ron, to the tiny harbour at Burwick, and you'll find a disused but still lovingly-maintained church building, known as Old St Mary's or the Lady Kirk. Step behind the pulpit wall into the small vestry and you'll find on the floor a stone about the size of a baby's bath in which are a neat, and quite deep, pair of footprints. And then, of course, take your pick of archaeological and historiographical theories about their owner, provenance, movement, age, and so on. But hey, we don't always need to be able to name the saints who pave our way, do we?

Other things plant themselves on islands, and not all are happy arrivals. If instead of driving South from the Hope

OH ALL RIGHT THEN

(as St Margaret's Hope is invariably called, and you can pronounce it 'Hop' or 'Hup' according to taste), I were to drive East to the appropriately-darkly-named Grimness, I would find on the shore just a little bit of an engine casing that used to be an entire ship now eaten by the sea. The *Irene* connects my two parishes in the most sombre way, for she was the merchant ship in distress that prompted the action of the Longhope Lifeboat on 17th March 1969. On that terrible storm of a night, the *Irene* eventually shelved safely on flat rock there at Grimness, while the eight crew of the lifeboat were lost in one of Britain's most famous maritime disasters. I mentioned one of the memorials to that incident in the story in the Introduction.

But I drive North towards the Barriers, hoping they are open. The story of Orkney's Churchill Barriers is well known. Following the sinking by U-boat 147 of HMS ROYAL OAK on 14th October 1939 in Scapa Flow, efforts were redoubled to prevent the enemy from sneaking again between the islands on the East side of Britain's vast natural anchorage. Block ships sunk in those channels (they variously date from both World Wars) had not prevented such a major tragedy, so something more drastic was required. Four concrete barriers were built in one of the biggest feats of engineering of the whole War, and still today carry the A961 from Mainland Orkney across Lamb Holm and Glimps Holm, into the lovely little community of Burray that forms the North part of my parish, and finally over to South Ronaldsay.[50]

The Barriers make us a unique community. Normally it doesn't feel like living on a small island, because *normally* you can drive to Kirkwall (Tesco and all) in 25 minutes from the Hope. In all but the summer, though, and far more frequently in recent years as the effects of climate change

---

[50] A fifth little causeway connects Burray to the small uninhabited island of Hunda. It was built as a test before the others, on a much smaller scale; but provides a surprise answer to the potential pub quiz question 'How many...'

are plain to feel, the Council and local police close the Barriers at the splashiest of high tides, and cut us off from everyone else. As you would expect, we have a ferry; however ours doesn't connect us to anywhere in Orkney, but instead to Caithness. And if the Barriers are closed no-one can get from the rest of the county to our pier, so the ferry is probably not going anywhere! (As I write this paragraph, that is exactly the situation.)

There is food for thought in that for ministry, and no doubt also for the school staff and the GP practice. To what extent is what we do self-contained? Since lock-down, it has been quite easy for people like me to exercise ministry (especially meetings) on-line; and if the electricity doesn't drop (and therefore the internet) in the bad weather, it's normally possible to keep working. And yet there is a touching sense of belonging, when the people I serve are marooned with me on this land mass, hoping none of us has a medical emergency because that will require the Air Ambulance to rescue us, and wondering how Doulls Shop and the Trading Post are doing for bread today.

Driving North takes me over the Barriers in reverse numerical order from 4 to 1. Between 2 and 1, as I cross the island of Lamb Holm, I see up a little road to the site of a WWII prison camp, Camp 60, which housed the POWs who worked to construct the Barriers. They were mainly Italian, which meant that initially they were working as prisoner-labour (my father, at the same time, was labouring on a farm estate in Silesia on the same terms, I suppose); but with the capitulation of Italy before the end of WWII, they eventually worked on a paid basis.

What you will see today, the sole surviving building from that vividly recent history, is the Chapel that was created out of two simple Nissan huts that sit end to end to provide a single space. By faith, art and ingenuity, a load of corrugated iron and lumps of concrete salvaged from the great engineering triumph outside were turned into a fake

Renaissance Chapel, one that always feels on the inside as if it is located somewhere that is sunny outside. When I bring visitors, I try to usher them in ahead of me, partly so that they can get the full effect of the interior unimpeded, and partly so that I can watch their reaction.

A short distance from the Chapel is another lump of concrete, this one a statue of St George slaying the dragon, to represent triumph over the suffering of war; there is often an Italian flag flying from the staff beside it. It's all known as 'the Miracle of Camp 60'. For me, the miracle is that any miracle would happen in such a completely unpredictable place; and if there then why not anywhere?

I know that the War Ministry still has me in its grip eighty years after the middle of the War as I drive North through the East Mainland of Orkney towards Kirkwall. The road has weirdly long straight stretches that undulate but only up and down not from side to side; and we're too far North for that to have anything to do with General Wade, whose calling-card that would be in parts of Highland Scotland. No, this is pure 1940s road-building.

Eventually, though, the switchback spits me out over one last hump, and I trundle down between the bonded warehouses of Highland Park Distillery and into our county town of Kirkwall.

The Mainland of Orkney consists of a large West Mainland and a much smaller and irregularly-shaped East Mainland, joined at a narrow isthmus on which the town of Kirkwall (Norse for 'the bay with the church in it') grew a thousand years ago. So though my journey will skirt the south edge of the town to continue my anti-clockwise tour of the shore of Scapa Flow, I pass not very far from the jewel of our medieval architecture, St Magnus' Cathedral.

What is the length of the history you visit at the tourist sites in your favourite holiday destination? In a town in Scotland they might manage something from the Wars of Independence in the thirteenth and fourteenth centuries, and something from the Wars of the Covenant in the seventeenth, so perhaps a span of about 500 years. Go to Egypt and they will manage a creditable couple of millennia from the earliest pharaohs to the Ptolemies. In Orkney we start from before the pyramids were dreamed of, with the oldest still-standing house in Europe at the Knap of Howar, running forwards through Iron Age brochs and on past the age of St Magnus and the building of the cathedral that honours him. But on still we go past the building of one of the finest renaissance palaces in Scotland (one of three palaces, by the way, if you can believe that for a place our size), all the way to that wartime history that is still remembered by old men who were nosey children spying on the Army from foxholes in the heather.

I guess, though, that the Cathedral[51] is the jaw-dropper out of all of it. Built of sandstone the exact colours of oddfellows sweets (I wouldn't last as a serious tourist guide, would I, but it's true!), it is a kind of girlie miniature of Durham Cathedral, with the same chunky romanesque pillars... only in pinks.

The story of its saint is extremely instructive. The thing about Magnus Erlendson is that he really was a Viking earl, and did his peacemaking stuff from inside that fate, not easy. For his story, you need to read many of the works of George Mackay Brown (1921-1996), Orkney's most famous modern poet, playwright, novelist and essayist. Essentially, though, Magnus' life echoed Christ's, as he chose a way of complete peace despite being born to the highest authority, accepted martyrdom with the courage of grace, and even[52]

---

[51] Fun fact: the Cathedral is not the church that gives the town its name. An older little church, one wall of which is built into a pend in the town, has that claim to fame.

[52] Centuries after Magnus' original burial on the tidal island the Brough of Birsay, his unmistakeable skeleton – don't ask why it's unmistakeable if you're at all squeamish – turned up inside a pillar in the Cathedral. It raised interesting questions about pilgrimage sites, and how prayer there really works.

defied attempts to keep him in a grave. He is a good saint to have, a proper saintly one.

Twenty minutes after leaving Kirkwall past its other whisky distillery, Scapa, I reach Houton with its two piers.

One of those piers serves the passenger launch that takes workers over to the oil terminal on the island of Flotta at the beginning and end of each shift. In its heyday the terminal serviced several tankers each week, but—as the industry is down-sized—it has reduced to just a few each month. We are going through a wonderful transition. Orkney is the early adopter *par excellence* of the renewable energy movement, providing world-leading facilities for the testing of tidal array energy systems, boasting an enormous use of EVs throughout the population, and embracing the possibilities of green hydrogen[53] which is being trialled in Council vehicles including some of the local ferry fleet. One possible future for Flotta might be in that last sector when larger scale hydrogen-fuel production develops. So when people come to Orkney expecting an out-of-the-mainstream and therefore rather out-of-date little place, they encounter some real surprises. I hope that when they encounter the Church in Orkney, their surprise is equally pleasant; to engage with what we are about does not mean stepping into a James Robertson novel – or for that matter a George Mackay Brown poem – any more.

The other pier at Houton is used by Orkney Ferries for the car ferry the MV Hoy Head, which describes a long thin triangle on the sea-chart as she plies among Houton, Lyness and Flotta, sometimes going clockwise round that route and sometimes anticlockwise according to the time of day and the busy-ness of each place. In the summer time the boat is chocabloc in the morning taking tourists over to Hoy and Walls, and again in the late afternoon bringing them back. They get their remaining pre-holiday cobwebs blasted out

---

[53] Hydrogen production is referred to by colour codes according to the residue created at production; green hydrogen produces no problematic residues at all.

of them as they stand up on the observation deck marvelling at the size of Scapa Flow and the scenery surrounding them… while Orcadian residents stay in their cars with the heating on and no view at all.

At Lyness, the visitor steps off the Hoy Head straight into the remnants of a naval base once home to tens of thousands of personnel. The physical remains of that dramatic little period of Orkney's history lie all around: fascinating, ugly, unmistakeable, dangerous, haunting. There are piers, chimneys, bits of railway track, a vast oil storage tank as big as a church. And amongst it all newer houses, families being families, a pub that still functions in one of the 1940s buildings, a fish farm company busily thriving, a museum with a pleasant day-time café. It feels as if our visitors look through the present without paying it a lot of attention – we all do that on holiday a bit, I suppose – and see the things of long ago… which the locals look right through or past as they focus on their here and now, their lives and loves and routines and needs.

My journey takes me South, past the modern school, past one of the island's much-loved church buildings (now preserved by a passionate local Friends Group), and then in a big curve round the end of the 'Longhope'. A 'hope' in Norse-influenced geography is a long thin bay, and you can work out that this journey is taking us from one hope to another, and that in each case the word has attached itself to the adjacent land (just as in English some towns have '-bay' endings to their names). So refer to 'Longhope' to an Orcadian, and they will probably assume you mean the little appendix of land at the far South end of Hoy and Walls, a peninsula attached to the larger island by an 'ayre', a causeway that takes the road round to the village that also takes the name Longhope.

OH ALL RIGHT THEN

And there you will find community in miniature, as you do in so many places in Scotland's Highlands and Islands. There is a small fire station, a small coastguard building, a small GP surgery, a small supermarket-style local shop, all perfectly-sized to serve a total population of 450. At the far end of the village lies one more gift from the past, a YMCA Hall now used as the biggest community space and buzzing with lunch-clubs, interest groups, entertainment and special gatherings of all kinds. Opposite the YM stands another of the island's three presbyterian church buildings, this one the very last to be released into local ownership. Beside it stands Kirkside, cosy Kirkside, unique – surely – Kirkside.

From the car I remove three things. One is a holdall with enough clothes for 72 hours; that's the 48 hours I expect to be there and enough extra to allow for the weather to catch me out for another 24. The second is a briefcase crammed with my worship materials for Sunday, the table-top tripod and levalier mic that will turn my mobile phone into the broadcasting end of a live-stream of the service back to South Ronaldsay, my desk-diary, laptop and charger so that I can do some work, and something to read in the quiet hours to come. The third item is a cool-bag with whichever of the contents of my home fridge I have decided might not survive my absence and need to be consumed while I'm here. When I unpack that last bag, I will discover in Kirkside's fridge or freezer a cake or ice-cream tub lovingly left there by the Reader in the congregation as their standard welcome to me. Maybe having told you that, I really don't need to tell you other things about those people, do I!

The sitting-room, with its new conservatory extension, will have been configured by the congregation for my comfort. That means that the sofa and a couple of armchairs and coffee tables will have been arranged near the window with the gorgeous view of the water of the Longhope, and when the day's schedule is complete, the

OH ALL RIGHT THEN

Hoy Head will glide past the window on her way to her overnight berth beside that of the Longhope Lifeboat. At the other end of the room, in that conservatory, are the communion table and its chair, the bookcase of worship materials topped with the telly monitor used for the live-stream, and – you are remembering of course – the ton-weight of font. Tomorrow morning all of these things, except of course the last!, will be re-arranged, and Kirkside will be ready for its congregation.

I wonder whether those saints of the New Testament who hosted the early church in the great cities of the Greek world felt the same way I do. Would the lady of the house have been asking her slaves to check that the kitchen wasn't too manky because the elders would be serving refreshments once the worship was over? Would everyone be assiduous in ensuring that the space reverted to its domestic tranquillity afterwards, with everything just as it had been in the first place when all was done? Did the head of the household stand at the door welcoming people he knew well, and feeling an extra little jump of inner pleasure when someone new tentatively appeared at the door as if they were not sure whether they ought to be there at all but hoping for the best?

Now you totally realise that I have described something that no other minister does in quite the same way as I do that journey and that ministry. You totally realise, too, that you could ask a dozen other ministers who live in rather distinctive places and they would spin you a yarn just as colourful and tell you just as many funny little facts you hadn't known.

I suspect that the number of ministries that are 'peculiar' is growing, because the Church of Scotland is having to become more and more creative in finding ways to minister to the whole of the country in terms of our constitutional responsibility to achieve that. Maybe every generation makes this mistake about the one before, but I have a feeling that ministry was probably less varied when I was starting out in it. There was an expectation about the relationship between a minister and a single piece of land, and between a congregation and a particular type of building. There was probably a rhythm and routine of ministry that could largely be transposed as a kind of template from one parish to another, varying a little between the urban and the rural but otherwise recognisable around Scotland. Now though, and increasingly in years to come, jobs will all have something notable and distinctive about them, and the matching of minist*er* and minist*ry* will be a delicate process of discernment of good 'fit'.

Sometimes there are lots of jobs available for the number of ministers and probationers who are looking for them; sometimes there are fewer. When the white-ripe fields are calling out to the few harvesters available to go to them, it used to be that you thought about the kind of place you wanted to live, where a spouse might work, where children might be educated, where you thought you could do most good and be professionally stimulated. You assumed, though, that beyond that the job was the job was the job. I think today, a minister seeking a call probably has to look at *every* parish profile they can find; for they will be looking at possible new lives that are mind-scramblingly different from each other, as the life of the whole ministry of the Church expands in more directions, shapes and colours than our predecessors could ever have imagined.

That, I suppose I've been wanting to say, is what Church of Scotland ministry feels like..

St Margaret's Manse, Orkney

Italian Chapel, Orkney

Printed in Great Britain
by Amazon

46917900R00108